COMING HOME

Born in the north of England, Maggie Hamilton moved with her family to New Zealand when she was ten. After gaining an MA in English Literature, she returned to England. In recent years she has been based in Sydney. *Coming Home* is the culmination of the last two decades of her own soul-searchings and discoveries. It is the journey that took her to the great deserts of the American south-west, to South-East Asia and to the ancient sites of Britain. Maggie now devotes her time to sacred journeying, and to giving talks and workshops.

COMING HOME

Rediscovering our sacred selves

MAGGIE HAMILTON

VIKING

Viking

Published by the Penguin Group
Penguin Books Australia Ltd
250 Camberwell Road, Camberwell, Victoria 3124, Australia
Penguin Books Ltd
80 Strand, London WC2R 0RL, England
Penguin Putnam Inc.
375 Hudson Street, New York, New York 10014, USA
Penguin Books, a division of Pearson Canada
10 Alcorn Avenue, Toronto, Ontario, Canada M4V 3B2
Penguin Books (NZ) Ltd
Cnr Rosedale and Airborne Roads, Albany, Auckland, New Zealand
Penguin Books (South Africa) (Pty) Ltd
24 Sturdee Avenue, Rosebank, Johannesburg 2196, South Africa
Penguin Books India (P) Ltd
11, Community Centre, Panchsheel Park, New Delhi 110 017, India

First published by Penguin Books Australia 2002

10 9 8 7 6 5 4 3 2 1

Copyright © Maggie Hamilton 2002

The moral right of the author has been asserted

All rights reserved. Without limiting the rights under copyright reserved above, no part of this publication may be reproduced, stored in or introduced into a retrieval system, or transmitted, in any form or by any means (electronic, mechanical, photocopying, recording or otherwise), without the prior written permission of both the copyright owner and the above publisher of this book.

Cover design by Louise Leffler, Penguin Design Studio
Text design by David Altheim, Penguin Design Studio
Typeset in 11.5/16 pt Fairfield Light by Midland Typesetters, Maryborough, Vic.
Printed and bound in Australia by McPherson's Printing Group, Maryborough, Victoria

National Library of Australia
Cataloguing-in-Publication data:

Hamilton, Maggie, 1953– .
   Coming home : rediscovering our sacred selves.

   Includes bibliography.
   ISBN 0 670 04038 X.

   1. Indian mythology. 2. Christianity. 3. Life skills.
   4. Buddhism. I. Title.

   291

www.penguin.com.au

*May these pages add strength and purpose to your quest,
and whatever thoughts are to be found here, hold them lightly
and weigh them against your own inner truth.*

*Embrace those ideas that strike a chord deep within.
And for the rest, simply pass them by.*

*And as you journey on,
may you embrace more fully who you are
and who you yet might be.*

For Derek,
the wind beneath my wings

Contents

Preface	ix
Acknowledgements	x
Introduction	1
The Re-enchantment of Life	7
The Awesome Gift of Human Life	11
The Kingdom of Childhood	17
The Human Quest	27
What It Means to be Human	34
Honouring Our Connections with Others	42
Nature's Bounty	54
Taking a Closer Look at Our Aspirations	64
Injecting Loving-kindness Into All That We Do	75
Discovering Our Own Sacred Space	84
Sacred Practices to Enhance Our Lives	94
Who Am I?	103
On Guidance	108
Where Do We Live?	116
What Is the Darkness?	125
Inhabiting Sacred Space	136
Entering the Silence	146

Uncluttering Our Lives	153
Attachment	162
Busyness	169
The Path of Harmlessness	177
The Gift of Forgiveness	185
Transforming Our Work	198
About Suffering	218
How Do We Love the Unlovable?	229
Understanding Our Emotions	237
The Value of Ritual	248
Living in the Magic of the Moment	259
About Death	267
Recommended Further Reading	283

PREFACE

WE ARE HERE ON EARTH TO WAKE UP
AND EMBRACE THE ADVENTURE OF BEING ALIVE.

For most of our lives we are gripped by the need to belong. We yearn to come home, to reach a space in which we are at one with our selves and with all that is around us.

And yet, while we spend a great deal of our energy searching for a place we can genuinely call our own, few of us find it. For too long many of us have occupied a space that is mundane, a space where nothing delights us any more.

In spite of this, life's profound beauty and magic are ever-present. All we have to do is learn how to recognise them so we can make them our own.

Human life is a remarkable gift. It is a journey back to self, to who we are in essence. Once we realise this we can begin to embrace the many possibilities that are ours and start to live each and every moment of our lives.

Home is where we belong. It is that place that defines and nurtures us, that allows us to be complete. We all have the capacity to reach our true home. When we do so, our life's journey will not be in vain, because we will then discover who we are and who we yet might be.

Acknowledgements

Nothing we create is purely of our own making – I owe so much to so many. Heartfelt thanks to my parents, Joan and Douglas, for the Light of goodness they have held for me through the years, and to Pam Sheldrake, who first had the courage to publish me. Thanks also to my many wise friends the world over who have loved and supported me in extraordinary ways. My thanks to Beverley Lichfield for her clear sight and guidance; to Juliet Rogers who gave me space when I needed it most; to David Parrish for his love, his Light and good humour; and to Lynda Collier who made my mountain sojourn complete.

I am greatly indebted to my dear friend and agent, Selwa Anthony, and to my excellent publisher, Julie Gibbs, whose confidence and vision mean so much. Thanks to my editor, Lyn McGaurr, whose guiding hand has improved my work immeasurably, and to the whole Penguin team for their commitment and enthusiasm. My thanks to Derek, my soulmate of old, who has lovingly supported my writing and my soul journeys with all the enthusiasm and commitment I could hope for and much more besides. My humble thanks also to the Great Spirit, my source and my strength.

INTRODUCTION

Most days our hearts are filled with intense yearnings, with dreams and schemes about how we might acquire that special something that will transform our lives.

Yet if we were to be granted our most profound wish, how different would our lives be? If in the blink of an eye we could realise our heart's desire, what would we ask for – the perfect partner, the big promotion, a decent bank balance, a happy family?

Whatever we seek is something missing from our lives right now. It is that special quality we hope will banish the overwhelming emptiness we feel deep within. Yet even as we contemplate our dreams coming true, experience tells us that these aspirations never satisfy. Sooner or later we will want something more. We will want to be acknowledged at home or at work, to purchase this appliance or those clothes, to have another holiday, to find our selves a new job, a new partner, and so the list goes on.

As we become aware of our many desires we begin to realise how much of our precious life's energy is expended on making our aspirations a reality. Already many of us have achieved a great deal, yet in spite of this, still our lives are filled with a profound longing. The more we have, the more we hope for, and the more strangely we need, until we find our selves trapped in a cycle of want that knows no end.

What if we were able to satisfy our soul's desire, to still the deep longing that visits us in quiet moments? What if we were able to step beyond all those things that limit us, and experience the deep magic of life? What then?

What we need most in our lives is not another job or relationship so much as the opportunity to come home to our true selves – to have the chance to recognise who we really are and what our brief earthly lives hold for us.

Our journey home to our true selves is the most profound journey we will ever make. It is the journey that will enable us to transcend our limitations and satisfy our needs – and access to all that is sacred is the key to making this possible.

It is hard to pinpoint exactly when the immense power and importance of the Sacred became apparent to me. Certainly I was blessed to spend my early years in the country with loving parents who understood well the profound nature of life. And even though the Second World War was still fresh in the minds of those around me, there was no lack of optimism. Friends and neighbours had a strong sense of the preciousness of life and of its deep magic. Still their lives were attuned to the natural kingdom, and all the great stories that had been handed down over generations were kept alive in everyday conversations. Time and again the old folk would recount their nocturnal encounters with loved ones who had passed on. Against this rich backdrop I would spend hours with my parents roaming the fields and woodlands, experiencing for myself the immense healing and nurture that is ever present in nature.

Although I suffered bouts of ill health and was confined to bed, I was never lonely. I learned how much joy and sustenance comes when we are able to have time alone with our thoughts

Introduction

and our selves. And while my formal religious upbringing was Christian, my parents exposed me to wider spiritual concepts, enabling me to see that the sacred laws of life are present in all good teachings. It is only as I look back I realise how much these experiences awakened within me an abiding sense of the beauty and sacredness of human existence.

Then, as the demands of everyday living took over, little by little the magic began to fade. There was school and university and then work. I was lucky to be successful in my chosen career, yet in spite of my success nothing could satisfy the increasing sense of emptiness I felt within. As I struggled to answer the questions that came to me in moments of silence, I yearned to find those things that would not only nurture and sustain me, but would make me feel complete.

There were many signposts along the way, but my first major breakthrough came when I learned to meditate. It was only then that I got a sense of the awesome space that lies beyond the pressures of daily life. This was not only a profound space, but the space where I belonged.

Inspired, I then began to read anything and everything I could lay my hands on, from the pioneering work of Raymond Moody on near-death experiences to Helen Wambach's accounts of life between lives. (For details of these texts and all others mentioned throughout the book, please see the 'Recommended Further Reading' chapter at the back of this book.) These books spurred me on to explore the landscape of life and of life beyond death. From here I discovered the works of many great teachers and thinkers including those of Paramhansa Yogananda and Paul Brunton and Carl Jung, and as I absorbed their philosophies I felt as if I was beginning to awaken from a deep sleep.

I began to attend group meditation sessions at the Siddha Yoga ashram, and here I became familiar with the beautiful teachings of Swami Muktananda, whose work grew out of the Hindu tradition. I also began to explore the basic tenets of Buddhism, appreciating the profound wisdom of these teachings. At the same time I was drawn to discover Native American spirituality, and I loved the expansiveness of this world view, and its celebration of the brotherhood of all living things. During this time I joined the local Theosophical Library with its remarkable collection of spiritual books, which proved to be a great source of works that had long been out of print.

Along with my reading and ongoing experience of meditation, I began to work on my sacred practice, and to seek silence and space. The more committed I became to these opportunities, the more my life began to flow. Still I was working and commuting and shopping and paying the bills, but in the midst of the everyday, remarkable things started to happen.

I began to meet people who shared my passion in the most unlikely places, and each of them inspired me, pointing me onwards, and further expanding my understanding and appreciation of life. Then without planning to do so I embarked on a series of life-changing journeys that took me to the great deserts of the American Southwest, through South-East Asia and to the ancient sites of Britain, where on each occasion another face of the sacred mystery of life was revealed to me.

It was in the desert that I gained a clearer sense of God, which has remained with me, transforming my understanding of myself and the world around me. For years I had struggled to give shape to the concept of God. Then I realised it is only when we let go of our many notions that we are more able to draw close to God, to the Divine Presence that lies within and beyond all things known and unknown. Throughout the book I refer to this expanded view of God as the Great Spirit, so that we might arrive at a more

INTRODUCTION

all-embracing sense of the magnitude of the Divine Presence. Yet even as I do so, I am aware that like all labels it too can only hint at what we seek to describe.

When I abandoned my need to define and contain God, and started simply to embrace the mystery of God, I began to get an intimate sense of the immense possibilities for our lives. I discovered that the inner and outer worlds are inextricably and profoundly linked. I learned also that the more we understand our own sacredness, the more everything in life has the potential to be a sacred opportunity – even those times that bring suffering and death. The more I worked with these understandings, the more the everyday aspects of life were transformed. Nothing seemed ordinary any more. I then realised that when we live with sacred intent we arrive at a place that not only sustains us, but enables us to be complete.

Often we imagine the journey to enlightenment to be full of pain and hardship, but it is life lived without this sacred intent that is fraught with disappointment and difficulty. Regardless of our present circumstances we are all here on Earth to embrace the adventure of life and to arrive at a full understanding of our own extraordinary potential.

We are here on Earth in the hope that we will succeed in our quest, and when we have the courage to embrace what is ours we will experience all the joy and assistance we could hope for. Once we can glimpse at the possibilities of our lives, we have made our first step on the journey home to our true selves. When we are where we are meant to be, doing what we love most, we are able to move beyond our fears and frustrations and allow our lives to unfold as they are meant to.

In setting down those things that have transformed my life, it is my fervent hope that we may gain a clearer sense of who we are.

The Re-enchantment of Life

Our search for meaning

Whether or not we realise it, every instant of every day truly magical moments are taking place. A child is born, a new leaf opens, we get the job we never imagined we'd be accepted for, we fall in love or we trip across some unexpected kindness and something deep inside us sings with joy. In this moment our endless worries and distractions dissolve. We find our selves absorbed in the present moment, and while we remain within this extraordinary moment we feel complete.

Then the experience passes, the old concerns return and our lives feel fractured once more. If only we could hold on to these special moments. If only life had a more permanent sense of peace and satisfaction, things would be different. That, however, is not our experience. Most of the time we are too weighed down with our worries to recognise life's magic, let alone experience it.

Yet in spite of this the supremely wise part of us knows exactly what we need to sustain us. This, our sacred centre, knows what feeds us body and soul, because it is the wellspring of our inspiration and the source of our own unique gifts. Our sacred centre isn't something outside of us, it is who we *really* are. It knows our most intimate needs and how to find them.

The problem is that many of us have come adrift from our true selves. We have forgotten who we are and why we are here. We have become confused and lost even. The physical world has not only become our one reality, it has become our prison, and the longer we are confined to this space, the less we are able to envisage what, if anything, might lie beyond it.

Deep down most of us long for a more satisfying existence, for a life that counts for something, yet often we continue to allow our selves to be ruled by our egos. We become preoccupied by what we can see and touch, by what people do or don't think of us.

Then when things go wrong we fall back on purely material solutions, because that is all we know. We distract our selves with sex and shopping, or with manic work lives, only to end up feeling even more empty inside. As our endless distractions lose their sparkle, we start to close our selves off even more from the things we need to make us whole, until our lives become little more than an ever-diminishing spiral of hopes and worries.

I am sure this pattern is familiar to us all. A friend loses a long-term partner or a family member gets retrenched, and terrified that this might happen to us, we try even harder to stay in control of our lives. We stop taking risks, stop being spontaneous, and without realising it we become imprisoned within the routine. We lose our ability to savour the tiny moments of happiness and in-sight and reflection that are ours to enjoy.

If we're not careful we end up expending our precious life's energy on trivial pursuits, in seeking questionable comfort from our achievements and possessions. Yet as exhilarating as these distractions might be, they do not feed our souls; they do not satisfy the hunger that gnaws at us in the moments of silence. When our physical lives become the sum total of our existence, we end up living as if we are purely physical beings. We end up living the lie.

Awakening to our many possibilities

No matter how confused we might be about our lives at present, our sacred centre is untouched by our fears and uncertainties, because it knows what we are capable of. It knows that first and foremost we are spiritual beings tasting the human experience, and so it waits patiently for us to wake up to our selves.

Whether we realise it right now or not, we are *all* masters and mistresses of our destiny, and once we have the courage to step outside the way we assume things have to be, we are then able to envision a better future for our selves and our world. When we have the courage to venture beyond our compulsions and our chronic busyness, a whole new way of being and seeing life reveals itself to us. When we wake up to our possibilities our sacred in-sight enables us to look beyond the way things are to the way things *might be*.

Somewhere along the way many of us have become so swallowed up in the process of living that often it is not until we have a major life crisis that we realise how truly mundane our lives have become. Only then do we bother to ask our selves why there seems to be so little joy in our days. Yet when we start to take a genuine look around us, we begin to see past the freneticism to another way of perceiving and experiencing life. Then as our gaze shifts beyond the literal, we realise we inhabit a rich multi-dimensional world full of mystery and wonderment.

When we reach this point it is a remarkable moment, because we are standing at the sacred portal of life, beyond which lies the place of all possibilities, and if we dare to shed our preconceptions and step inside, here lies more nurture, more in-sight, more peace than we could ever imagine.

<hr>

A thought for our journey: making life's magic our own

People will tell you there is no magic in life. What they are really saying is that there is no magic in their lives. The secret is to know that life's magic and beauty and wisdom are all around us. All we need to do is learn to recognise these qualities wherever we might be.

The Awesome Gift of Human Life

UNDERSTANDING OUR SOUL PURPOSE
The opportunity to experience human life is at an absolute premium, because it is here amidst the beauty and complexity of life where our soul's progress takes place. It is here against the extraordinary backdrop of deserts and oceans, mountains and forests that we are able to explore all that it means to be human and to learn from this experience.

That is why we are here clothed in flesh and blood, and that is why so many souls in spirit want to return to Earth. They long to gain the in-sight and soul development that is available to us here and now.

When we are feeling down it is easy to believe that nothing ever happens for us, that we are unlucky even. Yet already we have won the lottery of human life over countless souls still in spirit. Already we have what they long for – the question is what are we doing with it?

One of the reasons it takes us so long to get a sense of our life's purpose is because many of us have no idea what we are meant to be doing here. Nor do we have a sense of just how wonderful life can be once we do know our life's purpose. We are here on Earth to locate the Sacred, so that through this relationship our lives can have all the depth and meaning we yearn for. Put simply the more we embrace the Sacred, the more life's many textures will be revealed to us, and the more we will know our true selves.

As we begin to awaken to our potential, life's deep magic will reach out to us and provide us with what we need for our quest. We will begin to experience tangible improvements in our circumstances. For some these changes will be subtle, while for others they might well feel as if they are experiencing life for the very first time. This does not mean that we have to turn our lives upside down. Still we might continue to run a household, a local business or a corporation. The difference is that no longer will we be defined by these concerns.

Starting out on our journey of self-discovery

We can only begin our life's quest when we are able to move beyond our limited view of our selves. When we are open to the possibility that life can be different, our lives will be different. People and situations will start to flow around us in ways we have never experienced. Without even trying we *will* find our selves drawn to the things that are good for us. Even those things we find difficult will appear less so. As we open up to life we will find our selves being enchanted by the unusual and the unexpected, whether it be the impertinent bite of the wind on our cheeks, or the impossible beauty of the final moments of a friend's life.

Then as life continues to unfold we will get the distinct feeling that we are returning home. And the more we embrace this sense of belonging, the more we will find our selves starting to relax and to take things in our stride. Then as all the neediness and fearfulness that has dogged our lives begins to fade, we in turn will feel more able to genuinely embrace the world around us.

All this might sound simple – that's because it *is* simple. It is only our fear and our limited outlook on life that holds us back from reaching our full potential.

EMBRACING OUR OPPORTUNITY FOR ENLIGHTENMENT
The more we embrace the sacred beauty and wisdom of life, the more we will be filled with Light, because everything that is sacred is imbued with Light. And when every part of our being is filled with Light, then we too will become enlightened.

For most of us enlightenment doesn't happen overnight, but that doesn't make the journey any less worthwhile. We must never forget the journey towards enlightenment is the path to freedom.

When we embrace our soul journey we will find the experience an awesome one. Yet regardless of what happens, the secret is always to ensure our feet remain firmly planted on the ground. No matter what heights we aspire to, we must always remember to anchor our selves within the human experience. When we do so we will achieve all the progress we could wish for and much more besides. And so in amongst everything we aspire to at a soul level, still we must attend to the business of living. Before enlightenment we must collect water and chop wood, and after enlightenment still we must collect water and chop wood.

EXPERIENCING THE LIGHT OF OUR INNER BEING
As we gain more Light, our whole being becomes illuminated in every sense of the word. This is not just an uplifting process. This is the path that will take us home to our true selves, because each and every one of us is made of Light. Alberto

Villoldo describes this beautifully when he observes that we are Light bound into living matter. Many of the world's great myths and tales talk of advanced beings or of messengers radiating with Light – referring yet again to those souls whose inner radiance is unmistakable.

When we talk of Light it isn't merely a force for good, it is who *we* are. The Light is pure energy that has the ability to heal and uplift us and enable us to take control of our lives. The more Light we carry within us, the more we are able to transform each day of our lives into something remarkable.

Believe it or not, we will actually begin to *feel* lighter, because as we are filled with Light, all the thoughts and emotions and past experiences that have held us back will begin to slip away, leaving us free to travel lighter than we have in a very long time. If we were able to view our selves as we progressed we would see our selves radiating with an increasing amount of Light.

A dear friend chanced upon one of the great spiritual leaders of our time while travelling overseas. One moment this person was walking towards her in their body, and the next moment all my friend could see was pure Light. She had always respected this teacher, but had never had the opportunity to see someone who was fully enlightened before, and felt greatly blessed to do so.

This enlightening process is not just a pleasant notion, it is reality. That is why saints are depicted with gold haloes in medieval art and in icons. These are literal representations of the ever-present Light that surrounds highly developed souls, and this level of illumination is available to us all. Even when we find our selves in dire situations, the Divine Light of our being can and will illuminate our path, dispersing that which is unhelpful, because all those things that are dark cannot exist around the Light.

As the Light grows within us not only are our minds less

cluttered, we are also able to see people and situations as they are and not how we imagined them to be. And when we can see clearly what is around us, it is easier to see the way ahead. As we become comfortable with this new space, no longer do we fear the quiet moments, nor are we obliged to live up to the expectations of others. Instead we are able to focus on where we are heading, and on those things that will nurture and sustain us on the way.

The more we embrace life's sacred possibilities, the wiser we become. We will know when to inquire and when simply to embrace the mystery of the moment and allow it to ignite our passion for living. And as we honour the gift of our life and seek to inject it with all the meaning we are able, the more life's many dimensions will reveal themselves to us, enriching our waking and sleeping moments.

Our first step on this incredible journey of self-discovery is to develop a firm desire to connect with the Divine. Put simply our first step is to allow the adventure of life to begin.

A meditation touching life's magic

Find a place to be still, preferably somewhere you love to be. Settle down on a chair with your back straight and your feet on the floor. Close your eyes and begin to breathe slowly in and out. As your body softens and relaxes, continue to breathe slowly in and out as you recall a moment in life that was special in some way.

Allow yourself to experience the feelings and emotions you felt at that time. Observe how you felt in every part of your being. Note how the world seemed to you. Stay with these impressions and feelings for a moment or two as you recollect the visual images, the sensations and thoughts you experienced back then.

And now, as you gather up the richness of this experience, bring your attention back to the present. Breathing slowly in and out, hold this beautiful experience close. Take time to absorb it into every part of your being. Feel the beauty and wonder of it reaching out and touching you in ways you had never imagined. Know that you can always live within the energy of all the beautiful things that have happened to you, if you so choose.

Why not invite all the beauty you have experienced to be present in this moment? Ask that this beauty fill you completely. Then, as you feel yourself being filled with all this uplifting energy, ask that the sacred wonder of life be revealed to you each and every day of your life. As you remain bathed in this extraordinary energy, hold this intention firmly in your heart.

Then as you open your eyes take time to look around. Absorb every aspect of the space you occupy at present. Experience it as if for the very first time. As you stay in this moment know that when you can see deeply into all that is around you, there life's magic is also.

And now, as your attention returns to your breath, pause to give thanks to the Great Spirit for the gift of your life and for all the beautiful possibilities it holds for you.

The Kingdom of Childhood

Our birth is but a sleep and a forgetting.
WILLIAM WORDSWORTH, 'Ode: Intimations of Immortality',
Recollections of Early Childhood

KEEPING THE SACRED ALIVE IN OUR LITTLE ONES

No discussion of the Sacred is complete without some time spent on childhood. Of course we care about our little ones, and try to be the best parents we can. Yet often we become so caught up in our own search for meaning we fail to set up the circumstances our children need most to nurture their souls.

It is not enough that we feed and clothe and educate our children. They too need opportunities to explore and enhance the Sacred in their lives. Once we understand this, we can do a great deal to ease our children into earthly life.

When our children are born they still have a strong connection with the Divine – as Wordsworth noted, '. . . trailing clouds of glory do we come . . . Heaven lies about us in our infancy'. As our children grow we help them best by fostering this divinity.

Childhood is not just a precious time in our lives, it is an extremely vulnerable one also. Often we have no appreciation of just how tender a process childhood is. And when we have little sense of what our children need to enable them to stay connected to their sacred selves, we end up allowing them to live lives full of noise and distraction.

Without thinking we allow them to spend huge amounts of time in front of TV, where they imbibe millions of images that often overwhelm and disturb every level of their being. We allow them to become addicted to foods that are damaging to their bodies, to lead lives that are overly social and to become consumers almost as soon as they are able to take in the world around them. And then as their little lives are filled with endless toys and activities, we congratulate our selves for having done the right thing.

Parenthood isn't easy, and as much as we would love to wrap our children in cotton wool, they must live in the world in which they find themselves. As we strive to do our best, we must realise that not all unhelpful influences come from outside. Unless we are clear about where we stand, we too can end up neglecting the soul nurture of our children by infecting them with our materialism and boredom, because we are too tired and distracted to do otherwise.

Rediscovering the gifts of childhood

Sadly many of us have travelled far from who we were as children. We have become world-weary and cynical and full of doubt. Yet when we make time to be still, we realise how much we could benefit from the immediacy and innocence and the deep joy of childhood.

The path towards lightness of being is in part a journey back to the essence of our childhood – back to a more direct relationship with the Sacred and with the daily experience of life. When we are able to return to the fun and immediacy of this time, we are able to re-inject more joy and spontaneity into our days and thus enrich our experience of life.

As we contemplate these possibilities we are inspired to revisit the lives of our children. We can see how beneficial it would be if they were able to remain grounded in their sacred selves as they grow, so that they have a solid foundation on which to build their adult life.

Life in the womb

It is easy to forget how intensely sensitive, how aware, we are of all the energies around us in our infancy. Even when we are in the womb we are already starting to get a sense of the world in which we are about to live. Here it is that we first acquaint our selves with the major events that are taking place on the planet, with the feel and mood of the times. Over these months we are not only getting to know more of our parents and of all those who are part of our parents' lives, but about the circumstances in which we are to live.

I had first-hand experience of this some years ago during meditation, when without any warning I found myself back in my mother's womb. Not everyone had approved of my parents' marriage, and while I had been vaguely aware of family tensions, I hadn't realised how vehement they had been.

In that instant I became conscious of the family and friends around at the time my mother was pregnant with me. Not only was I aware of their thoughts and feelings, but of my reactions as well. Trapped inside my mother's womb I was subjected to this barrage of thoughts and words and feelings without any means of escape. I actually felt wave upon wave of unpleasant energy bombarding my foetal body as tangibly as if I had been dealt a series of blows. My response was to curl myself up even tighter in a vain attempt to protect myself from the thoughtless remarks that were being so freely aired.

When I came out of meditation I was as fascinated by the experience as I was shaken. There was no doubt that what I had seen was correct, because those who had made unhelpful comments were those who, in spite of their many kind gestures, I had felt uncomfortable with as a small child. Yet beyond my very human reaction to this situation, I was immensely grateful for this in-sight, because I then realised just how sensitive each of us is to the energies around us. More than this I understood how important it is for us to put aside our prejudices and reservations, so that from the moment we learn of someone's pregnancy we can make a conscious attempt to surround that developing child with all the Love and Light we can.

Assisting a new soul's progress into the world

We need also to be mindful of just how disorienting it is for a soul to be born. When we arrive on the Earth plane the experience is often a confusing one. In choosing to come here we have to leave behind the ineffable Light and refined energy of the realms of spirit. Then as we enter the Earth plane we enter an energy that is far heavier than we are used to. So trying is the adjustment to living here that it often takes the soul several years to acclimatise.

As our little ones battle the denser energies of Earth and the feelings of being helpless amongst strangers, it is vital we provide them with all the nourishment we can. When we can relate to our children as new arrivals from the world of spirit, we understand the importance of filling their lives with simplicity and beauty and space, and with everything that makes their tiny souls sing.

There are many wonderful aspects to contemporary childhood that we can enjoy with our children, but we must never forget that one of the most precious things about childhood is being able to appreciate the world from our *own* perspective and not from the packaged view of life that is so prevalent today. We can do this through the activities we provide for our children, through our prayers and through the sacred space we hold for them.

Dedicating our children to the Light

One of the best things we can do for our children is to surround them with Light. It helps to formalise our sacred commitment to them. Even though baptisms are often passed over today, they can still perform an important role in blessing a child's life and dedicating it to the Source of All Things. These sacred ceremonies also provide a spiritual focus for parents and godparents, and for friends and family, as they consciously commit themselves to assisting this child's journey to the Light. Even if parents are uncomfortable with a conventional religious ceremony, a sacred gathering can still take place with friends and family and godparents to dedicate this new life to the Divine.

Should parents have left organised religious worship behind, they need not rule out the opportunity to expose their little ones to one, if not more, of the great spiritual traditions. This then enables their children to receive a level of spiritual understanding around which they can then formulate their own awareness of the Divine. And if our children are able to spend time around those we know to be wise, all the better.

When we can do these things we help our children build a bridge between their own sacred space and the world in which they find themselves. When we ease their early lives by lessening the pain of alienation, we give them the best start possible to their earthly sojourn.

Understanding the alienation of childhood

Some children are able to adjust to life on Earth with ease, while others are very aware of the fact that no matter how intriguing this planet might be it is not their home. Some of my earliest recollections were of feeling alone in a landscape that was utterly foreign to me.

In spite of being blessed with loving parents, I can still recall the strong feelings of dislocation and the deep soul yearning to be back where I belonged. I felt as if I had been exiled a long way from home, and every part of me ached to be back there. Where home was I had no idea, but I knew the essence and feel of it. I also knew that one day I would return – it was the years in between that I didn't much care for.

One of the great consolations in those early years was my soul companion and spirit playmate, a magnificent lion that remained by my side night and day. His company was deeply reassuring for me. Never once did my parents question his existence, nor did they make fun of me. Instead they would kindly open and shut doors, and feed and take care of us both. I now know this spirit guide was sent to shepherd me through my early years, and I am deeply grateful for this.

I was blessed that my parents understood my soul needs and actively worked to nurture them. From my father I learned much about the healing power of plants, about the wonder and intricacy of nature, and about the miraculous web of life that binds us to each other. From my mother came exposure to a number of spiritual traditions. And from both my parents came the great stories – spellbinding folk stories, tales of spirits and sprites and other worlds, tales of life and death. So from an early age the many dimensions of existence were as real to me as the material plane.

Most important of all my parents honoured the presence of the Divine in all that we did. The sacred aspects of life were always part of our world, blessing our meals, our long walks, our holidays and our quiet times together. As I grew I thrived to know I was a child of the Great Spirit and that I inhabited a universe that was safe and supportive. I was well aware that life had its trials, but I also knew that in amongst the difficult moments there was great beauty and magic to be had as well. These were golden days and their deep sense of peace and stillness is with me even today.

Allowing our children time just to be

Too often we treat our young as if they are little adults, when nothing could be further from the truth. While our children are often wise beyond their years, they are still children, new arrivals in this strange and often bewildering place. All too soon they will leave the kingdom of childhood for the world we have created, so why not let them linger in that blessed space where there is great nurture and immense wisdom? When we can benefit from all the things that are good and beautiful and true as a child, then not only can we carry these qualities with us through life, but we can draw on them to sustain us in times of need.

We can also help our children greatly by ensuring they are not over-stimulated and over-supervised while they play. Naturally we must watch over them, but we must do so lightly and with great gentleness. If they are happy simply to play alone or to observe the world around them, perhaps that is what they need most. So focused have we become on the educational value of all that our children do that we have forgotten the immense importance of allowing our little ones simply to be.

The importance of nature

Apart from the kindness of my parents, one of the many consolations during my difficult early years was my intimate connection with nature. We lived in the country so I was able to spend hours playing alone in the garden, feeding on the gentleness and deep nurture of nature. I was blessed to have all the space and tranquillity I needed to flourish. For me even the faerie kingdom was but a heartbeat away and I would spend hours gazing at flowers and seeking out the faerie folk.

When I was a little older we would walk for miles through the woods and meadows, enjoying the natural beauty and the characters that lived around us. The beauty, the silence and space fed me, allowing me to adjust to being here on Earth at my own pace and in my own way. And so I was able to begin to absorb the rich tapestry of earthly life without pressure or distractions.

Access to nature might not be so easy for those living in cities, but still we can walk in the park and take occasional trips to the country. We can share the many nuances that come with each day, each season, and can gather up feathers and stones and shells. Still we can watch the sun and the moon as they cross the sky. The ways to enjoy the sacred beauty of our world, and our selves, are infinite.

Once our family moved into town our lives changed, yet still my mother made the effort to do many wonderful things. In winter she would buy my sister and me a potted bulb, which we kept in a warm place and watered with care. Then after some weeks came that extraordinary moment when the first green shoot appeared through the soil. When finally this single bulb was transformed into a sweet-smelling hyacinth we were thrilled, and to this day I love hyacinths. These are the kinds of simple moments that can touch us profoundly.

The value of those who are older and wiser

If we hope to enrich the lives of our children, it helps to surround them by those who have depth and substance. It is beneficial for them to mix with differing generations, to be with the elderly and with those whose cultures are different from our own. We can introduce them to their ancestors through family photos and stories. And as we seek to enrich their lives, we mustn't forget the great stories and myths that have fed the hearts and minds of countless generations. These are the stories that inform and inspire, that teach us about the quest – about good and evil, and about the way things are as opposed to the way things seem. These timeless stories teach us about hope and about honouring our selves and others, about responsibility for our actions and inactions. These are the tales that enable us to hold a mirror up to who we are, so that we can glimpse at who we yet might be. These are the tales that feed every part of us, that point to the ultimate hopefulness of life. They inspire us to keep on going, to dare to be different and to dream.

Helping our little ones discover their own sacred space

As the joy of life becomes more apparent to us, no longer is it hard to keep this energy alive for our children. As we cultivate our own close connection with the natural kingdom, we can more easily communicate its beauty and wisdom to our children. Then, as we discover those places that are sacred to us, we can share these with our children, so that they too can begin to discover those places that are sacred for them. The more we drink deep from the well of life, the more we are able to teach our little ones to do likewise.

So as we seek to nurture our young, as we strive to make their little lives as full and as rich and as blessed as we are able, we come to realise that the kingdom of childhood is for us all. When we honour it in our children, we honour it within our selves also. As we do so we enhance all the magic and beauty and Light on this tiny planet of ours. In so doing we then experience the deep soul satisfaction that comes when we are able to help other souls to journey home.

Contemplations on childhood

Find somewhere you can be alone with your thoughts. Then, as you allow your breath to slow and your attention to return to your body, take a little time to contemplate some or all of the following:

- What are the gifts from childhood that my life could benefit from right now?
- How can I create a sacred space for my children at home and in the world?
- Who are my wise ones whose wisdom my children can benefit from?
- How can I best honour those who have passed over with the children?
- What space do we need as a family to allow the Sacred to be more present in everything we do?
- How else might we invite nature into our days?

THE HUMAN QUEST

*We are not human beings having a spiritual experience;
we are spiritual beings having a human experience.*
PIERRE TEILHARD DE CHARDIN

UNDERSTANDING WHY WE ARE HERE

The absolute miracle of our lives is that we *are* here on Earth, and that long before we were born we made a conscious choice to be here. Assisted by those who are far wiser than us, we made this choice on the basis of what we needed most for our souls' growth, and part of that decision was who our parents were to be, and what race, culture and sex we were to experience.

Even though we might be born into the same family or neighbourhood each of our life situations is different. This is because our personal circumstances were designed to help set *us* free from the limitations of material life and from all the things that at a first glance seem so real. In short, the situation in which we find our selves here on Earth has been crafted to enable each one of us to achieve our full potential.

This does not mean that everything in our lives is predestined. What we do with our lives is up to us. Sometimes we are wise in what we choose, but often we make decisions without much thought or in order to please others, and then we wonder why our lives are so unfulfilling and frenetic most of the time. If, however, we had used our innate wisdom in the choices we have made, then many of our frustrations and disappointments would not have eventuated.

Free will is ours
Each of us has the freedom to fly like an eagle or to live a life that is diminished. Whichever path we choose is up to us. No force on Earth or beyond it can take this away from us unless we allow it to. We can choose to live like sleepwalkers, never questioning why we are here or what we could do with our lives, or we can grasp the extraordinary potential earthly life offers us and see where it takes us.

Living each and every day of our lives
Human life was never meant to be a series of tests we have no hope of passing. Rather it is an infinite kaleidoscope of opportunities tailored to bring out our innate abilities. We are here to make the most of our life physically, mentally and spiritually. We are here to experience life beyond the limitations of being clothed in flesh and blood, so that we can escape the endless roller-coaster of hope and despair. This is the journey. This is *our* journey.

The miracle of love
When we choose to take this incredible human adventure seriously we will come to understand many things, none the least of which is that love in its highest form is the most powerful force in the universe. And if we want to get the most from our brief lives, we will take the time to explore the quality and texture of this love that is inside and all around us.

This kind of love isn't sentimental or emotional or falsely modest. This kind of love is exceptional – it is the means by which we are empowered to be who we really are. When we are able to reach out and make it our own, we too will become exceptional at every level of our being.

We can begin to grasp the shape and texture of this remarkable love when we watch a mother tend her newborn child or when we observe those who risk life and limb to give help to those in need. The nature of this greater love comes to us in those supremely happy moments when we feel truly cared for, or when we witness human triumph over incredible odds.

Some of us might well have been fortunate enough to experience this greater love during meditation, or in the presence of a divine being. When we do so we are absorbed into an ocean of love so vast that we lose all sense of who we are apart from this love – for that extraordinary moment we return to the essence of who we are at our most sacred. This love doesn't have to be an experience we have once or twice in our lives. It can be ours each and every moment. Where there is a genuine willingness to embrace this kind of love for our selves, wisdom and in-sight will follow, pointing us forward and enabling us to make this awesome love our own.

Living the lives we do, it is sometimes hard to understand how we might make this greater love a reality in our lives. Often we don't feel remotely wise or genuinely loving, and so we assume this kind of love is not achievable or perhaps we fear that if we were to give in to love of this magnitude it would demand too much of us. We can't leave the job or the kids and go and live in a cave or an ashram, and so we assume we are stuck with life as we know it.

Yet it isn't the getting of love we should fear so much as the lack of it. When our lives are starved of love we inhabit a place of limitation, of doubt and faded vision. And all these irrational fears and notions do is keep us chained to the treadmill of never-ending activities and achievements where one week dissolves into the next, until it's not just weeks but whole decades of our lives that have slipped by.

How different our lives would be if this greater love were ours right now. When, however, we stop for a brief moment and let go of all the busyness and all our concerns and contemplate this kind of love, it makes our hearts soar to think of it. But how do we get there? The secret to making this quality of love our own is in being able to stretch our imaginations beyond life right now, to how it might be if everything we did and experienced were informed by this greater love. This is important because our thoughts are powerful beyond belief – they create the world we live in. So as we contemplate the possibilities for our lives, let us begin by dreaming the big dreams, by allowing our selves to move beyond all the stress and the pressure, so that we can begin to create the kind of love in our lives that will feed us body and soul.

LETTING GO OF OUR FEARS

Where there is love that is real there is nothing to fear, because it sets us free. And when we can move beyond our fears and feelings of inadequacy, everything around us readjusts itself. This is the power of our intentions.

Then, as we begin to let go of old mind sets, we will find our selves breaking out of the routine, the familiar. We will find life responding to our new expectations. We might well find our selves re-evaluating those people we dislike, and to our surprise we will often discover they aren't as bad as we imagined. We might discover we actually like them, and can no longer see what there is to dislike. We might also find our selves embracing new jobs or leisure activities, and being delighted by how much enjoyment they bring us, or rekindling good friendships we have allowed to fade. As these new ways of living begin to work for us, we will find our selves more willing to surrender our need to control each and every situation. Instead we are able to enjoy more spontaneity, so that each day becomes more of an adventure and less of the same old routine.

COMING ALIVE

When we begin to recognise *who* we are, we realise that hidden deep within our seemingly ordinary selves lies someone extraordinary. As we begin to wake up to our extraordinary selves, we also awaken to the wider beauty of life. The more wonder and beauty life holds for us, the more we are able to love. The greater our capacity to love, the more we are filled with Light. Once we understand this, we are inspired to enhance the Light within us and to make it the foundation on which to build our life's quest.

As our experience of life becomes more expansive, the more we are able to lead lives that are rich and rewarding. Without even having to think about it we find our selves striving for those things that elevate the human spirit. Then, as we continue to expand our appreciation of the beauty and intricacy of life, we discover that there is no detail in our lives that is too inconsequential when viewed through eyes that can recognise the Sacred. We then realise just how profound the love and support the universe gives us is – we understand what the Master Jesus meant when he said that even the hairs of our head are numbered.

Often we become so clouded that our daily lives are little more than a relentless round of back-breaking activity and sleep. When, however, we start to open up to the love and beauty of the universe, all kinds of astonishing things will happen when we least expect them. A number of years ago my husband and I holidayed half a world away on a remote island that was accessible only by a two-hour canoe ride. For weeks I had dreamed of lying in the sunshine and playing a tape of my mantra (our mantra is a sacred word or phrase that might be given to us or chosen by us). When we reached our destination, I discovered I had left my tape at home. A couple of days later we met Chris who came from another part of the globe altogether. Although we had barely spoken, he insisted I borrow one of his tapes, which turned out to be an exquisite recording of my mantra. Chris had no idea of my spiritual aspirations, let alone my mantra, nor that I had left my tape at home. I was greatly moved by this little miracle – it is one I will never forget.

As we start to experience this extraordinary love and support in our everyday lives, we are then motivated to make it an integral part of how we live. This means holding on to positive outcomes and reflecting these qualities in all that we say and do. Once we allow the Divine to inform our life's quest, we are then able to move beyond the paralysing effects of the past and into a whole new way of living. No longer do we need to wait for the clouds to open before we inject new meaning into our lives.

When we are consciously connected to our divinity, we are anchored in that which will never fail us. The ever-constant nature of the Divine is like the peerless blue of the sky. Regardless of how the skies appear from the ground, above the clouds the skies are always perfectly blue. The same is true of all that is sacred – in spite of all the disturbing things that can happen in life, those things that are numinous within and around us remain untouched. They are there for us to access once we know where they are and how we reach them.

The human quest offers us the opportunity to let go of the minutiae and peer beneath the surface of everyday life, so that we can discover all the wisdom and in-sight that awaits us there. Knowing this we are then able to glimpse at the extraordinary possibilities for our lives and to give thanks for them.

A prayer for guidance on the quest

'O, Great Spirit, help me to honour the absolute miracle of my life. Help me to embrace my life's quest with courage and joy. Help me also to transcend the concerns of daily life, so that each day I might in some small way be touched by those things that are sacred. And as I strive to become intimate with all that is sacred, may I also grow in wisdom and love as I journey home to my true self.'

WHAT IT MEANS TO BE HUMAN

Your spirit is part of God and all Knowledge lies within you.
WHITE EAGLE

STEPPING OUT OF THE DEAD ZONE
Being here is not a dress rehearsal. This is it. Yet often we are so preoccupied with our everyday lives that we have no sense of what we should be doing with our selves beyond our jobs and our relationships. When we switch off from the wider possibilities that life offers us, we're not really living, we're surviving.

If we want to experience all that our life has to offer, we need to learn how to inhabit our bodies and our planet joyously and meaningfully. This isn't always easy, especially for those of us who live in towns and cities. It is hard to feel alive when we work in airconditioned buildings under artificial lighting – so used are we to controlling our environment that often we avoid the heat and the cold and the wet. And as we don't have to grow our own food, we don't take much note of the weather or the seasons either. We don't even have to mix with others if we don't want to.

While this way of living might seem convenient, it is also detrimental to our life's quest, because all of these things are in our life for a purpose. They have the capacity to centre and uplift us and to teach us a great deal. When we divorce our selves from our human experience, we diminish the opportunities this lifetime offers.

At some level most of us are aware that our lives are on hold. We know we are living in a kind of limbo, waiting for the perfect time to get moving. The problem is that if we keep waiting for the waves to part before we can experience a new and vibrant way of life, odds are we will end up waiting forever.

Learning to live again

We can only ever fully embrace our human adventure when we are able to genuinely inhabit our bodies, when we are literally earthed. *Now* is the time for us to shake off our lethargy and find interesting ways to make each day worthwhile. We can begin by starting to take note of everything that is going on around and inside us. There are many ways we can do this, but few are easier than making the effort to walk, because walking helps ground us in our bodies.

This might mean getting up a bit earlier to take an early morning walk or putting aside time to walk in the evening. We might like to think about taking the stairs at work instead of the elevator, or choosing to walk part or all of the way to and from work.

Reaching out to the world around us

When we walk we are not trying to prove anything – we are learning to *be* – and so our walking should be relaxed with our arms hanging easily by our sides. As we walk, it is important we do so in silence, so that our walking becomes a contemplative experience. By allowing our selves the luxury of quietness, we allow our minds to expand. Then we are in the right kind of space to be, and to be inspired. When we have settled into our walk, we can then contemplate what it means to be here on Earth, experiencing all that we do.

Once we start to open up to the beauty around us, and to take in the immediacy of this experience as we walk, we cannot fail to be energised and uplifted. Then, as we allow our awareness to expand, we can start to take note of the ground beneath our feet, and to register this is Mother Earth we walk upon. Without the Earth we would not survive – day in day out it feeds and heals and supports us, whether we appreciate it or not. Knowing this, how can we fail to be moved by the sustenance we receive?

Then, as we start to look more deeply at other living things around us, we will begin to enter a profound relationship with these forms of life as well. No longer are they objects to be noted or appreciated, but living breathing plants and trees and creatures of every kind, which are also seeking to thrive on this tiny planet of ours.

If we allow our experience to deepen as we walk, we will begin to feel a genuine part of each day. We will find our selves noting the distinctive scent of dry earth in late summer, or the hint of wood smoke on the cold night air. We will begin to notice the colours and textures of the trees, and the sweep of the ocean. And as we continue to absorb these things, we will start to become aware of the effect that each of these living things has upon our being, and to realise how profound a relationship we share with everything on the planet.

We might well find that we develop an intimate relationship with certain birds or trees or rocks. When this happens these living things will start to reach out to us, and if we are respectful they will share their wisdom and their love. It is through these very relationships that we have learned the healing properties of plants and trees, and of those places that naturally uplift us, mind, body and spirit. We might even develop a relationship with a particular species of bird or animal that becomes our protector and teacher, and that appears when we least expect it, surprising us and uplifting our spirit when we are sad or weary. These are the profound nuances of life that await us, and when we can awaken from our distraction, we too can drink deep from the waters of life.

Aliveness is what our human quest is about

The more we establish this sense of connection with life, the more we will be inspired to embrace life. We can experiment with this in many ways – by walking barefoot in the garden or on the balcony on a cold winter's morning, just to remind our selves we are alive. If we can't get outside, we can stand for a moment or two on the bathroom tiles, or take cold showers during summer. These are just a few of the exhilarating ways we have to start the day and to celebrate the joy of being in the here and now. All these things are important, because they allow us to feel the lifeblood within us. They enable us to wake up and remember that we are here on Earth.

As we start to become aware of our physical selves, we will find our selves opening up to myriad experiences that would have previously passed us by. A number of years ago I took up African tribal dancing. As my feet pounded the Earth's surface I was energised by the music and the dancing. Then over time my awareness shifted to the ground beneath my feet, as I slowly became aware of the greater heartbeat of life that existed beyond my own. This was a profound realisation and as this connection with the Earth grew, it proved to be deeply healing.

INVITING LIFE'S MAGIC IN

As we go about each day we can teach our selves to see into the heart of things, and to express our gratitude for everything no matter how seemingly inconsequential. As we bathe we can give thanks for plentiful water in which to relax and refresh our selves. As we eat our breakfast we can note the taste and texture of our food, mindful of all the life contained within our food – of the sun and the rain and the fresh air that has made this food possible. We can spare a thought for all those who have worked to bring us this food – for those who tend the fields and drive vast distances, and for those who stock the supermarket shelves. Knowing all the effort it has taken to bring us this food, how much more delicious is it?

As we dress we can give thanks for our clothing and for the roof over our head. Stepping outside, we can consciously breathe in the air, and take in the rain and the sunshine. As we walk down the street we can observe the people and the buildings, the trees and the cars, so that again we are present in the moment, feeling what it is like to be *here* on planet Earth, to be part of these surroundings.

When we are able to move beyond our distracted way of living and reach out and touch all those things around us that are as alive as we are, we enter the realm of the Sacred. This is the deep magic of life that awaits us all.

A meditation celebrating the gift of life

Sit or lie in a comfortable position. Breathing effortlessly, close your eyes and slowly bring your attention into the room, and then into your body. As you breathe in and out, take note of any parts of your body that feel tense and allow them to relax. Straighten the spine and allow your shoulders to drop.

Then, as you follow your breath in and out of your body, take a moment to contemplate the breath of life as it carries oxygen to the many millions of cells in your body. In and out the breath flows whether you are aware of it or not. In and out it flows on the days when you want to dance with joy and on the days when you are filled with despair. In and out the breath flows when you feel close to the Divine and on the days you do not. In and out the breath flows, bringing your body the life it needs to support your human quest.

Take a moment to feel the life force entering your body. Feel it filling every cell of your body with life-giving oxygen. Pause now to contemplate the gift of human life, the gift of *your* human life. This incredible vehicle is home to your spirit. The miracle of it! Know that you are blessed. You are blessed. You *are* so blessed.

As you sink deeper into the consciousness of your body, with your eyes still closed take a moment to allow your fingertips to touch. As you absorb this sensation, give thanks for the gift of touch, for this precious gift that enables you to feel the presence of a loved one, to enjoy the warmth of the sun on your skin. Yes, you are well and truly here on planet Earth, in a wonderful vehicle that lives and breathes. You are blessed. You *are* blessed. You are so blessed.

Now, with your eyes still closed, allow your fingertips to explore the skin on your hands and arms and legs. Experience now the miracle of your skin that holds together all the many bones and organs and muscles and veins and arteries in your body.

Then, as you bring your fingertips up to your face, take a moment to explore the skin of your cheeks and forehead and nose. As your fingertips linger over your face, allow them to trail gently backwards and forwards across your eyelids. Housed within these lids are your eyes, your precious eyes through which you view the world with its many textures and shapes and colours. You are blessed, are you not? You *are* blessed. You are so blessed.

Then, as your fingers move slowly down your face to your lips, experience the different texture of your lips. It is through these lips that you take in the food and drink you need to nourish your body. It is through these lips that you express your love and communicate with the world. What a miracle this is.

And now, as your fingers touch the many creases and folds of the skin of your ears, you are reminded of the precious gift of hearing – of the ability to hear the cry of a newborn baby or hear the comforting voice of a friend. What a gift is your ability to hear. You are blessed, are you not? You *are* blessed. You are so blessed.

Then, as you return your hands to your lap, contemplate for a moment the richness of the human experience that you carry with you each day of your life. Take a moment to give thanks for every cell in your body, for the miracle of sight and sound, of touch and taste and smell.

This is the awesome gift of human life, and this vehicle that is intricate beyond all imagining is home to your spirit. This beautiful body is the cocoon inside which your sacred self resides, so care for it well, knowing that you are blessed. You *are* blessed. You are so blessed.

And now, as your heart expands with joy and gratitude

for all that you have, take a moment to give thanks, heartfelt thanks, for your life as your fingertips explore the wonder of your body once more. Run your fingers through your hair, trace the shape of your jaw, trail your fingers down your throat, your chest and stomach, and around your waist to the curve of your hips and buttocks, then down your legs to your toes. Let your whole being reflect on the miracle of life, of this, your life, and the body in which it resides.

Return your hands to your lap and bring your attention back to your breathing. Observe the flow of breath in and out of your body. Take a moment to honour the Great Spirit in making the gift of human life possible. May this life bring you great in-sight, great peace and joy, for you are blessed. You *are* blessed. You are so blessed.

Then, as you continue to breathe in and out, may you carry with you this profound reminder of the gift of your life. May the days and years you inhabit this body be greatly blessed, and may your human quest hold all the in-sight and love and wisdom possible.

Honouring Our Connections with Others

We are here on a quest for the getting of wisdom
How then do we begin to tap into the many possibilities that each of us has within? How, in amongst earning a living and bringing up the children, do we make our human experience count?

The more we learn of our selves and the world around us, the wiser and more loving we become. We are here on an extraordinary journey that enables us to discover that we are part of everything that has ever been, is now and ever will be. Even time and space cannot limit who we are in essence, and our human quest is the gateway to this knowledge. It is here in our interactions with others that we learn about our selves and all we are capable of.

Understanding our need to belong
It is no accident that a good deal of our time is spent in exploring our relationships, because at some level we all have a deep need to belong. The problem is that often we waste a lot of time and energy trying to discover where we fit in, not realising that *already* we are part of everything around us. The more we

understand our place in the great web of being, and the sacredness of this connection, the more we realise that any feelings we have of isolation are just an illusion, because we can never be separate from the great sacred family to which we belong.

Most of us want to feel part of those around us, yet often we can't quite seem to make this happen, and when we have tried to reach out, often we have ended up feeling disappointed or disillusioned. We have become so used to our anonymity that we have forgotten what it feels like to belong, and while we long for meaningful relationships, we spend our lives focused on other things. Then, as our lives become stark and uninviting, we retreat and so our isolation grows. We convince our selves that our essential loneliness serves us well, and if we are not careful we end up focusing in on our selves, until not only do we become the central player in our world, we become the only player.

Sadly many of us have too few meaningful relationships. We have become so caught up in our jobs and our security that we have stopped spending time and effort on those around us, not realising that the realms of deep joy and profound in-sight are rarely to be found in those things we have worked hard to achieve or possess.

The deep magic of life comes to us fleet-footed, carefully concealed within everyday people and places. It is visible to those who have learned to see beyond the obvious.

OUR JOURNEY BACK TO BELONGING
Re-establishing our connectedness with life is essential for our soul's progress, because it is here in the *midst* of life that we learn more about who we are and who we yet might be. Imagine how lonely we would be if we were to undertake this journey without

other people around us. It is hard to imagine what this might be like, because we *need* each other.

When we are feeling down it is easy to bemoan the fact that our lives seem ordinary or unglamorous, because no one buys us flowers or takes us on expensive holidays, yet the more we fixate on such details, the more we fail to appreciate what is already good and true in our lives. We fail to treasure the partner or friend who does love us, and who will take the time to paint our apartment or care for us when we are sick.

These are gestures that are real. These are the loving touches that add to the quality of our lives. And so when we cease to notice others or to acknowledge them for all they have done for us, we fail to experience the satisfaction that comes with being human – with being able to laugh and cry, and to celebrate and commiserate with those we love.

No matter how solitary or dysfunctional our lives might have been, there is *always* a way back to belonging. We can make a start by waking up to the many good relationships that already exist in our lives and by honouring them as well. This might well be the love of a partner or close friends. Equally it might mean giving thanks for the upbeat person that greets us at the news-stand or the local café, or someone we see regularly at the bus stop or train station who always has a pleasant word. All these connections are important, because they add shape and texture to our lives.

Gathering up all the good the past has given us

How different our lives would be if others had not been there for us with their encouragement and their kindness. We can get a sense of the exquisite possibilities of this when we contemplate a loving moment we have already experienced in our lives as children and as adults. As we begin to look back, in spite of all our battles and disappointments we can see how much our lives have been sustained by the accumulation of all this love.

This isn't just about being grateful for the many good things that have happened in our lives, but about gathering up all the Light we have gained from the kindness of others and making this an integral part of who we are. Once we are able to acknowledge this love, we are able to gather it about us like a cloak, then anchor it deep within, so that we can carry all this loving-kindness and nurture with us into the future.

This is a profound opportunity for us, because when we do gather up all the Light we have experienced in life, we not only enhance the Light in our lives, we *become* the accumulation of all this Light. Then even our past takes on a different hue, because in amongst our difficulties and disappointments we begin to see the absolute gift that so many people have been to our lives and we realise how much is already ours to enjoy.

Discovering what feeds us

As with all that is sacred, the benefits are manifold – the more Light we possess the more loving we are, and the more our world becomes a safe place. When we live within a loving space, all sense of dependency and neediness fades. We are better able to accept others the way they are, because we feel complete.

The more we anchor our selves in the completeness of Divine Love, the more we are able to genuinely love others and to feel joy in their presence, and the more our observations of those around us deepen as well. Still we are able to see their fragilities, but we are motivated to try to see them as completely as possible, knowing we are *all* works in progress. And as we look at others more closely, we will find our selves in absolute awe of the unique qualities that those around us bring to the world.

Making contact soul to soul

When we do seek to appreciate all those who love us, this is not a superficial or sentimental act, but one that acknowledges those around. When we can relate to others at a profound level, we begin to see them at their most sacred – we start to see their very souls. And in seeing who they *really* are, we set them free from any limitations we might have placed upon them. Being able to see those around us in this way is a sacred privilege, and one that will transform our interactions with others.

Inspired by these possibilities we will find our selves actively seeking ways to make genuine contact, so that we can touch that which is supremely sacred within all we meet. When we do so, we touch something far more intimate than any sexual encounter, because we are touching life at its essence.

A contemplation recalling those we love

Why not bring to mind someone you love dearly? Take a moment to look at them as if for the first time. Feel your heart expanding as you observe their hair, their skin, their mannerisms, their turns of phrase. Remind yourself of the unique qualities of their voice and their touch, their outlook and their life's story. There is much you have stopped noticing, and yet the wonder of it is that still this person loves you and cares about you. As you absorb their love, feel the immense joy this person brings to your life in every cell of your being and bless them for it.

Learning to love lightly

As we honour those who have loved and cared for us, and give them all the encouragement and support we are able, we must always do so lightly because we each have our own journey ahead of us. So, as profoundly as we might love someone, the true test of our love is when we do not cling to them in any way.

When we are able to hold those we love lightly, something inside us all is set free. This is the stuff that changes lives, because the more we let go of our attachment to others, the more life's opportunities come to meet us. Put another way, the more we pray for the enlightenment of others, the closer we come to our own perfection.

Holding on to good outcomes

Not everyone who comes into our orbit will return our goodwill. While this can be disappointing life still requires that we continue to be compassionate and respectful to all we meet. This doesn't mean we are less discriminating, but that we are less likely to pre-judge outcomes and arrive at hasty, frequently incorrect conclusions.

Often the reason we don't get on with others is that they don't seem to like us – they might be distant or abrasive, so we take offence, and the unhappiness grows. As we learn to work with the Light, we learn to live less subjectively and are thus less likely to take offence. Instead, when we can inject good intentions into a situation everyone benefits. Life can be impossibly hard when we feel we can never measure up – many of us have experienced this as children and as adults and have been diminished by this. When, however, someone touches our lives with kindness or inspires us to new heights, we are lifted out of our everyday selves and can achieve many things. Once we realise the capacity we have to help others, we can begin to hold a good intention for them also, knowing that goodness is simply another form of healing.

If we allow our selves to be sustained by the immense power of the Light, this ability to hold on to good outcomes comes more naturally to us. As a result, we no longer take selfishness and unkindness in others so personally. Instead, we look deeply at the troublesome situation and see that person's inner pain, and in seeing this we are able to behave more judiciously, knowing that our goodwill can and will dispel the darkness of ignorance and fear around this situation. We can hold the Light for another, no matter how trying the circumstances, thereby illuminating their path and encouraging them on to their highest good.

When we practise patience, compassion and respect, we activate the deep veins of healing for our selves and others, and everyone wins, because life becomes easier for all concerned. Once we understand the awesome power of the Light we are no longer tempted to take part in actions that diminish our selves or others, because we now know that when we hurt others we hurt our selves.

In the past many of us have performed kindnesses and have been hurt by the lack of recognition we have received. This happens, but it is wiser not to be upset by this. Some people are more aware than others, and so always we must focus on the worthwhile nature of a particular deed, rather than on the need for praise and commendation.

Often we have no idea of the impact we have on someone else's life. The person in question might not realise what is being done for them at the time, but that is insufficient reason not to be kind, not to be generous even. A dear friend of mine who is well able to communicate with souls in spirit says that one of the most moving aspects of her work is in observing how overwhelmed those who have led good lives are when they pass over, because they had no idea how great the impact their everyday acts of love and kindness had been on others. Not only are these souls able to witness the effects of their Light, they are able to experience the accumulation of all this Light as well. We too are able to benefit greatly from the Light we accumulate.

When we approach acts of loving-kindness without thought of reward, the more our caring will return to us many times over. Then even the humblest act of service can be a sacred opportunity. In ancient times even sharing food was considered a deeply sacred gesture. Where then is the Sacred in our daily interactions with others?

EVEN THE SMALLEST KIND GESTURE CAN CHANGE LIVES
As we become more intimate with the sacred beauty of life, we realise the power of the most simple acts of goodness, because it is the *intention* not the act that is important. There is a beautiful story living saint Mata Amritanandamayi (Amma) tells of a man who was walking along the street, when his day was transformed by a stranger's smile. Encouraged, the man went off to his usual restaurant for lunch. Carrying the innocent warmth of the smile with him, he was prompted to give the waiter a generous tip. Overjoyed, the waiter then gave a poor man some money to buy himself a meal.

Some time later the poor man bought himself some food and shared it with a hungry dog. Once they had had enough food the pair headed out of the city and travelled on until night closed in. Needing shelter, the poor man knocked at the door of a house, requesting permission to rest on the veranda overnight. The family not only allowed them to sleep on the veranda, they gave them a meal as well.

During the night the house caught fire. All would have perished had the dog not raised the alarm. The poor man helped the family from the house and fortunately no one was harmed. Years later the youngest son of that household became a great spiritual teacher who transformed the lives of thousands.

Who would have thought a smile could have such a profound

effect? It makes our spirits soar to contemplate this. And although most of the characters in this story were never aware of the final chapter of this happy tale, it doesn't matter. What matters is that each person was a link in the chain of greater good.

As we begin to explore our connection with others, our lives will come into balance and a new quality of peace will descend. It often feels as if the sharp edges of life are being slowly rounded off, so that even the more painful aspects of living are less keenly felt. And then no longer do we have the desire to win at the expense of others. This doesn't mean that we lose our sense of purpose, but that life no longer holds the same terrifying intensity we had become used to.

Each time we connect positively with another, we become more human. Paradoxically we also transcend the limitations of material existence, because the more love and compassion we can share with others, the more we touch our own divinity and the Divine in all things.

Lighting the path of another

There are many ways we can bless the lives of others. One beautiful way to help someone is to imagine that person bathed in the soft golden Light of the Divine. Then, as we hold this image, we can imagine them being wrapped in a love so great that it defies description. We can then ask that all that happens to this person be for their highest good. This can and does work. Try it for yourself.

It is wonderful to extend this kindness to strangers, or to those we see on the news who are lost and frightened or suffering. And as we give out this loving-kindness we are reminded that whatever brings Light to one life brings Light to all.

A meditation honouring those who have loved us

Find yourself a comfortable spot where you have a pen and paper to hand. Then, as you close your eyes, settle down and become aware of your breathing. Allow your mind to be still. Follow your breath in and out of your body; feel yourself relaxing. If any tension remains, allow it simply to dissolve as you continue to breathe in and out.

Now it is time to reconnect with all those who have warmed your life's journey. How long ago it was that they encouraged or helped you doesn't matter. Time and space have no relevance here. Even death presents no boundaries for you to honour all the many blessings you have received.

Start by recalling some of the loving gestures you enjoyed during childhood. Not everyone was kind to you back then, but as you concentrate on this time a whole range of people come to mind. Some you hardly knew, some you haven't thought about in a long time, but here they all are. Who would have thought so many people would have touched your life, encouraged you, in some way? Your heart expands at the thought of it.

Now, as you focus on one of these many people, take a moment to recall the positive experiences you shared with that person. Relive the moments of joy, of unexpected kindness. Recall how good it felt to have that person in your life. Feel the extent of their love, their support. Experience the immense lift you gained from their loving-kindness. You may want to recall a number of incidents involving this person. Allow yourself time to relive these moments. Allow your whole being to bathe in this love, for this love is real and it is yours to keep.

As you take a moment to visualise this person more clearly why not recall some of their unique qualities that surprised and delighted and challenged you? Then, as you feel your heart expand with love and gratitude, thank them for all that they have given you.

See them standing before you in your mind's eye. And now, take their cheeks in your hands and gaze deep into their eyes, knowing that as you do you see their very souls. Make contact with them at their most profound level and feel the love they have given you flowing out from you back to them. See them surrounded and suffused with Divine White Light. Envisage them cocooned in this Divine Light. Now pause to kiss them gently on the forehead, and give thanks for their lives. Ask that all they have given out be returned to them many times over. Ask that their lives be greatly blessed and that all that they do be informed by this sacred Light.

You can now move on to another person or to another chapter of your life, or you might prefer to stay with that particular person for now. It is tempting to rush this process, but the best results come when you spend a little time with each person in turn. When you're done it might be useful to write down each person's name and a few words that best describe what they have given you.

A prayer in closing

'O, Great Spirit, I give thanks for my life and for all those who have eased my life's journey with their kindness, their love. And as I honour them, I glimpse at that greater love towards which I am journeying. Help me to gain a greater sense of the sacred connection I share with all things, and may each and every day of my life be a blessing to myself and others.'

Nature's Bounty

It is no accident we are here on Earth
We have talked about a world without people, but our tiny jewel of a planet is far more than a collection of people and nations. It is a landscape of jungle and desert and woodland, populated with billions of plants and animals. So much a part of our lives are these living things that it is impossible to imagine our world without them.

The very act of agreeing to be here means we have chosen lives that connect us with all living things, yet for most of us our connection with the natural world is tenuous at best. Some of us have had so little contact with nature that we have come to fear or distrust it or even to ignore it. And so we cover the Earth with concrete and crowd out the skies with buildings of every kind, and then wonder why we feel so out of joint much of the time.

Unabashed we tamper with the genetic and chemical structure of our world. We slaughter animals without respect for the fact that they give up their lives so that we might thrive. So divorced are our children from nature that we have to take them to zoos or to farm days at shopping centres for them to have contact with the animal kingdom.

Where then is our gratitude and our respect for this magnificent planet and all upon it that sustains us daily? Where is the humility and the understanding and the wisdom that reminds us that we are only part of the great pattern of being? Not only have we forgotten who we are, but we have forgotten the profound sacredness of all that surrounds us. We have forgotten that everything we do individually and collectively comes at a price, and ultimately the price isn't dollars and cents but the expansion or contraction of our souls, the destruction or preservation of our planet.

When we do seek to connect with the natural world, it is often less about trying to be part of nature than it is about understanding what we are already part of. Whatever contact we have with the natural world can be immensely valuable and deeply healing, but realising the full significance of what we are connected to is most important of all.

Embracing the deep lore of existence

Many of the world's indigenous peoples can teach us a great deal in this regard – they understand well their relationship with nature and respect it deeply. For them the plants and animals, and indeed all living things, are part of the sacred web of life, of which they too are members, and whenever a life is taken they honour this sacrifice, taking only what they need at that time. There is nothing naive or simplistic about this view of life. It is a profound way of living, because when we understand that a deer or a wolf is a family member, one's relationship with that living creature cannot help but be different.

How easily our environmental problems would be solved if we were able to hold such attitudes. No longer would we feel free to exploit and abuse and slaughter the animals we do, or to pollute our skies and waterways without thought. Instead the natural world would be ours to nurture and respect, and in return we would be able to experience the deep joy that a genuine connection with nature brings.

When we honour other life forms, we honour our selves

Every living thing on Earth seeks to thrive and be happy, and if we are genuine about embracing the Sacred, then we must honour all life, because we are all part of the greater whole. Where life must be taken, it must be done with the utmost respect and gratitude. As we come to understand the absolute preciousness of life, it becomes our soul pleasure to respect the right to life of other life forms and to protect them.

There are many practical ways we can show other creatures our respect – when we see a spider, instead of killing it because it frightens or annoys us, we can simply acknowledge its right to live and see that it is put outside. If we have pets we can take care never to hurt them, but strive to respect their dignity and their needs. Then as we go about our days we can give thanks for the deep and enduring sustenance we gain from nature. When it rains, instead of grumbling as we reach for the umbrella, remember that it is the rain that waters the crops that sustain us.

When we enter into the natural rhythm of life we are able to appreciate these things so much more. We can see the plants and the trees thriving in the mists and the rain. In seeing these things, that part of us that connects us with all living things thrives also. Whether we are at this stage of connectedness with the life around us or not doesn't matter. We need only remind our selves what it feels like to slake our thirst when we feel parched to get a sense of the exhilaration the plants experience when the rain closes in. Or we can appreciate what it feels like for the great forests and the grassy plains when the rain falls by recalling how good it feels to us to take a shower at the end of the day – to feel the water washing over us, soothing and refreshing and cleansing us.

We are all part of the perpetual movement of energy that never dies

Once we are able to connect with the natural world we are able to benefit from its vibrancy, from all it can teach us and from its healing touch. There are times in our lives when we feel uplifted and times when we feel we are stagnating. Yet the natural world teaches us that no matter how things might appear, we are never in a state of limbo. We are all part of the movement of the wind and tides and planets. Even within seemingly inanimate objects the dance of life goes on – in the great mountain ranges, in the rocks and the boulders, the atoms move about as freely as they do in our own bodies.

When we understand this, then even when we are feeling stuck we can begin to move beyond our impatience and our despair and recognise that at some level things are taking place in and around us. Nothing need ever be lost on us. Instead of fretting about when our lives will have more momentum, we can simply allow our selves time for reflection until the wider pattern of events is revealed to us.

The desert is a great teacher in this regard. At a superficial glance nothing seems to be going on, but then as we look more deeply all manner of riches begin to reveal themselves. We discover the desert is teeming with life. The same is true within us. While we might feel as if we are inhabiting an internal desert, when we look deeply we will see this is far from the case.

When we embrace our belonging, we heal our sense of disconnection

As our consciousness expands, we can not only see a tree, but we are inspired to run our hands over its bark and to hear the whisper of the wind through its leaves. Or we can sit for a few moments with our backs to its trunk as we begin to experience the nuances that are available to us when we take an interest in the many living things around us.

Then, as we gaze up at a tree, no longer is it just another tree, but a unique life. In seeing this we are able to feel joy in the way this particular tree grounds itself in the earth or in the complex pattern of its leaves that shade us from the heavens. As we run our hands over rocks and stones, we begin to sense the vitality that exists beneath our fingers.

Anyone who has been to one or more of the many sacred standing stones that still exist will know how distinctive is the energy in each stone circle, and how different the energies emanating from each stone within a particular stone circle. These are deep understandings that the wise ones have always known – long have trees and mountains and stones been hallowed and cared for. This is why there were sacred groves and standing stones – these special places were conscious attempts to enhance the exceptional energies that were already housed in certain trees and stones and locations.

Those who have gone before us were great observers of the natural world. For them the signs of nature were part of a common language and of experiencing the world. Even my father's generation was able to read the weather with astounding precision. They could tell by the flight of a bird whether a storm was brewing, or whether there was rain on the wind. There is no great mystery to these things. When we take time to contemplate the world around us, the natural kingdom will reveal its wisdom to us in all sorts of ways. And then we are able to enjoy the many lives that surround our own.

Embracing the rich bounty of the seasons

The seasons have much to teach us, literally and symbolically. Winter is the return to the deep, black and inviting nurture of the womb. It is a time for withdrawal, for contemplation and rest and dreams, as we forsake the cold outdoors for the warmth of our hearths and homes. And even though the world might seem stark and inhospitable, winter is the time to contemplate.

It is the time to be inspired and to gain in-sights that will inform the next phase of our life – in-sights which will take us beyond our present contemplation to future action. If we embrace the opportunity for retreat that the chill of winter brings, we will find our selves drawn into those forgotten parts of our selves from which new sources of strength and purpose can flow.

If we fail to recognise what winter has to offer, we can end up remaining frozen inside. And when we are frozen there is no chance of in-sight or growth. If we are to benefit from the wintry chapters of our life we have to learn to sit in the stillness and to embrace the seeming barrenness of this time, so that we might be drawn deep inside – into the very heart of our inner being. Only then can we garner the wisdom that resides within us.

Then, as the days begin to lengthen and the dark of winter recedes, once more we are drawn outside of our selves. As the sun warms our days we begin to take a wider view of our selves and our world. We begin to sense the many opportunities available to us.

Spring is the time when we begin to let go of the past and to reinvent our selves as the world comes to life again and we connect with our innermost dreams. As we venture forth from the darkness of winter, instinctively we move towards the Light and towards a new level of being out in the world. Spring is a time of great beauty and of unpredictability also. It is a time to travel forward with care as we emerge out of the introspection of winter. Progress we must, but we would be well advised to make haste slowly.

Then, as the days grow warmer still, summer overtakes us and once again our lives have a sense of expansiveness and greater ease. It is a time when many of us feel most relaxed about our selves and the world around us. We are inspired to open up, to be out in the world and to be with others, so that we can share the bounty and abundance of life.

Summer is a joyous season because it is the time when our blessings and our growth are most apparent to us. It is a time when the sheer vibrancy of life warms our hearts and spurs us on. And yet as exhilarating as summer can be, we need to take care, because if we expend too much of our energies in the outer world, just as when we spend too much time in the sun we can become burnt and dehydrated, so too we can become drained and distracted when we get so busy we forget to rest. In summer we must always balance our desire to be out and about, with time to replenish.

Then as the light turns to gold and the leaves are tinged with rust, we pause to contemplate Earth's bounty and to rejoice in her fullness. With the falling of the leaves comes a sense of the near completion of another cycle of our lives. And as we consider everything that this cycle has brought us, we give thanks for all that we have received and learnt.

In the midst of our contentment there is a poignancy also, for the wheel of life must keep on turning. No matter how complete our journey might feel, always there is room for greater understanding, greater wisdom. And so once more we are drawn towards a time of introspection, of becoming still. As we prepare to retreat from the cold and dark of winter, we must have the courage to allow those things that no longer serve us to drop away. When we watch the trees shed their leaves without effort, we too learn the effortlessness that comes when we are able to leave the past behind us.

Many blessings await us when we take the time to absorb the sacred wonder of life, and as we explore the beauty and complexity of creation, let us always tread lightly. Let us treat all the living things who share our planet with love and respect, so that every day some new aspect of the sacred mystery of life will be revealed to us.

Rejoicing in the miracle of a new day

Having been inspired by the possibilities ahead of us, where do we begin? It helps to start with the dawning of a new day and all possibilities that it brings, because how we start the day informs the tenor of our lives. It is easy to haul our selves out of bed in the morning and drag our selves through the day without any real awareness, and then wonder why our lives lack the significance we seek. When we allow our selves to be swallowed up by busy schedules, one day blends into the next, until our whole lives slip past in a blur of activity, devoid of any real joy or meaning.

The ancients took a different view. For them the dawning of a new day was a sacred experience, a distinct moment in time to be savoured. As the sun rose above the horizon it was an opportunity to give thanks for the ongoing gift of one's life and all that it might bring. It was the time also for contemplation, and so each day was begun mindfully, with a definite sense of the sacred opportunities that were available to those who sought them.

When we take the time to welcome each and every day of our lives, what a difference it makes to our wellbeing. Honour the new day as an untouched page in the ongoing story of our lives, then each day will have a tangible sense of adventure about it.

A meditation honouring the dawning of each day

On rising, why not make physical contact with the day by stepping outside or by simply standing by an open window? Breathe in the morning air and take a moment to acknowledge your connection with all things. There is nothing as delicious as the first breath of fresh air in the day. Savour it and know that as you do so you are breathing in the very breath of life. And as you become more aware of your breath, give thanks for your life.

Take in a slow, deep breath through your nose and consciously breathe in the love of the Divine Presence. Feel this love entering every cell of your being and infusing it with Life and with Light. Allow this Love to flow through you, as you ask that it be anchored deep within you. Feel it transforming your whole being. Then, as you breathe out slowly and fully through your mouth, ask that through this same love your life will benefit all living things.

Take a second slow, deep breath through your nose, and consciously breathe in the peace of the Divine Presence. Feel a profound peace entering every cell of your being, infusing it with calm and with Light. Allow this peace to flow through you, as you ask that it be anchored deep within you. Feel it blessing your whole being. Breathe out slowly and fully through your mouth, and ask that through this same peace your life will bless all living things.

Take a third slow deep breath through your nose, and consciously breathe in the wisdom of the Divine Presence. Feel this timeless wisdom entering every cell of your being and infusing it with in-sight and Light. Allow this wisdom to flow through you, as you ask that it be anchored deep within you. Feel it illuminating your whole being. Then as you breathe out slowly and fully through your mouth, ask that through this same wisdom your life will illuminate the lives of all living things.

When you have completed these few simple breaths, take a moment to absorb your surroundings. Raise your eyes to the heavens. Feel the bite or caress of the air on your skin. Listen for the piercing cry of a bird or the low moan of the wind. Absorb all you can without effort or judgement.

Then, as you take one last look around you, contemplate all the peace and love and wisdom that this as yet untouched day might bring. Now it is time to go forth and embrace the Light of your own true self, so that by the end of the day you may leave the world better, wiser, more loving than you found it.

Taking a Closer Look at Our Aspirations

Our deepest fear is not that we are inadequate.
Our deepest fear is that we are powerful beyond measure.
It is our light, not our darkness that most frightens us.
Author unknown

Understanding our need to succeed
From birth we struggle. We struggle to walk, to read and write, to gain an education, to come to terms with the world and other people. Then as we near adulthood we rejoice to be free, only to discover that a whole new set of responsibilities and expectations are required of us. And not wanting to disappoint, we begin to run with the pack – their values become our values, their aspirations our aspirations.

At first it feels good to be part of something beyond our selves, until we discover that we are constantly having to prove that we have got what it takes. The more we do so, the harder it is for us to imagine life beyond these compulsions. Then, as our personal vision fades, our goals become little more than a never-ending list of things we must do or have. When we think about the future we consult our diaries instead of our inner vision, until we become trapped within a lifestyle that is laden with expectations.

Taking a Closer Look at Our Aspirations

We all want to be successful, but how do we arrive at our own definition of success when daily we are presented with images that define success for us? What, after all, is harmful about a new pair of sunglasses, a new suit or a new car? The game is fast and the rules change constantly. It is easy to get swept along with questionable values, simply because we are too distracted to do otherwise.

Our intentions are our karma

If we hope to succeed on our quest, we need to be mindful of the goals we set for our selves, because they inform the direction and quality of our everyday existence. Everything we are and yet might be results from our thoughts and ambitions.

So what of our intentions? Are we genuinely trying to live our own lives, or are we trying to live up to the expectations of others? We live in a world that is driven and moving so fast that there is almost no time to reflect. So skilled are we at processing huge amounts of information and responding to the many stimuli around us that our capacity for in-sight and wider vision has become severely impaired. If we're not careful, we end up simply reacting to whatever is before us.

What in the moments of silence do we yearn for?

If we hope to see our way clear, we need to determine what qualities we want from our lives. Most of us would like to feel that we have sufficient depth to seek things that are of worth, but rarely is this borne out in our lifestyles. We yearn for peace and in-sight and for a real sense of joy, yet most of us spend our lives securing the next outfit or relationship, and the next. And when these things fail to thrill us, we distract our selves in wine bars and shopping centres, or in front of the TV.

Rediscovering the magnificence we carry within

The reason for much of the confusion we experience in life is that we are strangers to our true selves. In spite of all our education and sophistication we have no idea who we really are. One popular story tells of a great kingdom under threat. Living in that kingdom is a child whose life is hard and whose identity is uncertain. As events deteriorate a search goes out to find the one who possesses the unique gifts that can save the kingdom.

Only when the worthy citizens are near despair do they discover the one they seek is the child that no one paid any attention to. It is within this young stranger that extraordinary powers lie – powers that can vanquish the darkness and restore the kingdom to peace and prosperity. And when finally the child is recognised and allowed to fulfil their true destiny, they succeed in saving the kingdom. Then the child receives the recognition that is duly theirs.

This is a hugely satisfying tale, because we can all relate to the terrible loneliness of the one who is unrecognised, to the isolation of mind, body and spirit experienced by us all on the human quest. And when the identity of the child is finally revealed we are overjoyed, not just because this is a good story, but because this is *our* story. We too are exceptional. Within our seemingly ordinary selves lies that which is extraordinary. We too need to recognise our true selves. We too must fulfil our destiny.

Coming home to our true selves

Here we are, adrift in this beautiful yet alien landscape, strangers in a foreign place, wondering who we really are and what we are doing here. We can spend our whole lives searching for things to fill the emptiness within, or we can embrace our quest. The choice is ours. Sooner or later we will finally realise that our mission is to discover our true selves. In spiritual terms this is referred to as the shortest journey, because all we seek is already within us, and when we have the courage and in-sight to access our inner divinity, we will find that we too are unlikely heroes and heroines capable of many things.

We can only begin to access our sacred selves, however, when we create space in our lives for our thoughts and, more importantly, *between* our thoughts. The guidance that comes from the soul comes to us in that space that lies beyond the hype and chatter, and when it speaks to us, it is a voice that is like no other. It moves us to the depths of our being, touching the very essence of who we really are.

Discovering our own inner voice

When we start to allow some space in our lives, we are then able to begin to determine what *we* want from life. We can begin to shape our own unique vision and to dream our own sacred dream. Within the stillness we learn to distinguish between our inner voice and the many voices that seek to drive us daily. And as we do so we learn that our inner voice is that intuitive part of us that prompts us towards actions that are for our highest good, that brings us clarity.

When we listen to our inner voice we gain in-sight – we obtain access to the wisdom we carry *within* us. We are all born with this deep inner guidance. It was given to us to help us on our quest. We can only benefit from it when we use it. Whatever our inner voice tells us, we can be assured it will deliver the very best outcome possible. The direction given might be left of field, but as we learn to trust our inner voice we will discover there will also be an extraordinary sense of rightness about this information. Frequently the guidance we receive will be disarmingly simple – so simple that the immensity of what we are being told will not always be immediately apparent to us.

When we approach our inner voice for direction, we must do so with a genuine willingness to listen and to be open to what we are being told. Then and only then will we receive the illumination we need. Always we must honour the sacredness of this opportunity. Then, as we look into the heart of our situation, we will be able to see more clearly what lies there.

This isn't about drowning in our thoughts and notions, but about looking deeply at a particular situation and peeling back the layers of what is apparent to us, so that we can see what lies underneath. Once we have this in-sight, we are in a far better position to decide what we should or should not do.

There will be times when the answer to a problem isn't immediately apparent to us. When this happens we need to remain where we are in life, until the full meaning of the situation is revealed to us. This isn't always easy for us – so addicted are we to outcomes it is hard not to react. If, however, we have the courage and tenacity to remain still, we will save our selves a lot of unnecessary heartache.

At one stage, a company I was working for went through a merger. We knew it wasn't going to be a straightforward process, but none of us had any idea how impossibly hard it would be turning up for work day after day, knowing that people were going to lose jobs, knowing that everyone's lives were being turned upside down. Colleagues in rival companies took delight in capitalising on our inevitable shortcomings, in making life harder. There were many decisions we were able to influence, but there was also much we had to accept.

The guidance I received made it clear that no matter how tough things got I was to stay until the fullness of the experience was revealed to me. This was the last thing I wanted to hear, but trusting the guidance I stayed, mindful of the fact there was clearly more I had to learn. As it turned out there was much I gained from that time. I couldn't make everything right, but I could try to be compassionate and respectful towards everyone concerned. During those years I made many friends, I spread my professional wings and enjoyed the challenges that came with my new brief.

Regardless of whatever goals we set our selves, it is the deep soul learning and the ability to honour others along the way that are central. It is here amidst the complexities of daily life we discover the true source of our strength. We also learn what we can change and what we cannot, and how to direct our life's energy and Light accordingly. Then to our delight we discover that through such times can come great strength and in-sight, and much more besides.

Choosing what we want with care

Embracing our life's quest is not a matter of living mean little lives, but about choosing only those things in life that will enable us to take flight. This means that we must take care what we wish for, lest we get what we want. The great myths and fairy tales are full of stories of those who have been granted their heart's desire, only to find that it is not what they wanted after all. Whether it is King Midas, who turned everything he touched including his food into gold, or a friend who chooses a highly paid job over one they are passionate about, the message is the same. We each make our choices and have to live with the consequences.

Always we need to guard against being overtaken by personal ambition and by self-aggrandisement. We don't need to do things that are unworthy to succeed. No matter where we are in life, we still have the capacity to positively affect the lives of those around us, as well as contribute to our own soul's progress. If we do harness the wisdom we hold deep within and allow it to inform our endeavours, who knows what impact our lives might have at a national, corporate or community level?

Discovering the source of our aspirations

When we begin to examine what we aspire to, we need to ask our selves *who* it is who wants these things. We need to determine whether we are dealing with the never-ending demands of our ego or the promptings of our soul. We need to ask our selves one of the most profound questions: 'who is the "I" who seeks this or longs for that?'

If we make decisions based on our ego, we will find our selves dancing to everyone else's tune. Our ego is the chattering, flattering voice that gnaws at us daily, that is concerned with self-preservation and with what others might think or say. It is the voice that drives us to be selfish and self-seeking, to do or say things that are unworthy. Always the ego will seek to undermine our inner voice and all that it seeks to tell us. It is not the 'I' that will serve us well.

Life is a very fluid process

There are so many opportunities awaiting us in life that it is madness to limit our selves to one way of doing and seeing things. This is about daring to step outside the square that has been prescribed for us, about having the imagination to wait and see what might happen, and the courage to take flight when the perfect moment arrives.

When we are able to follow the path of the soul, life's profound magic will present itself to us in ways and at times we can't even begin to imagine. The more we are open to these possibilities, the more they will occur. Then to our surprise we will learn about a new job through a chance conversation with a friend, or we will find a new home by taking the wrong turn on our way across town.

Life will always have its times of uncertainty and its moments of sorrow, but underpinning this will be a tangible sense of being looked after. We are not placed here on Earth to struggle on in the vague hope that we are heading in the right direction. There is more guidance available to us than most of us realise. We are literally surrounded by beings of Light, who wait for the moment when we are ready to accept their assistance.

When we begin to embrace the enormousness of who we are, we are ready to embrace the fullness of life in all its manifestations. So no matter how overwhelming life might seem, we are then able to rise above the challenges of the moment and recognise that there are many opportunities to be had. When we understand this our vision expands, as do our horizons, and we become a more genuine part of the world in which we live.

So as we begin to readjust our ambitions to accommodate our most profound dreams, we realise that true power doesn't reside in those who run corporations or countries even, but in those who understand what they are here for, and have the courage to embrace their unique quest.

A meditation honouring your own voice

Each name holds its own unique vibration, as does each letter in that name. When you name something you give it form, so when someone changes their name, they alter the energy around them. Often those who enter sacred orders take on a new name to mark their change in vocation. The women's movement also recognised the right of women to keep their own name as an important aspect of their self-empowerment. To keep your name or change it is your choice.

If you are to step into your own personal power, you need to learn to honour who you are. One of the ways to do this is through honouring and celebrating the energy and sound of your name.

Find a place where you can be alone, where it will be no problem to make as much noise as you need to. You might like to stand or sit for this exercise. Once you are comfortable, take a moment to become quiet. Follow your breath in and out of your body as you bring your attention back inside. Then, as you feel yourself begin to relax, check your back is straight. Allow your shoulders to drop and the muscles around your eyes and your jaw to soften, as you continue to follow the passage of your breath in and out of your body.

Feel your attention settle deep inside, then take a moment to ask the Great Spirit to be with you as you seek to embrace more fully who you are. As you feel this loving presence in and around you, become aware of those times when you have given your energy away to people and situations that are not helpful to you. Recognise these leaks in your personal power and begin to draw back those parts of yourself that you have given away.

See these lost parts of yourself returning. And as they become part of your energy once more, wrap them around you like a cloak, until you are cocooned inside your own energy. As your energy settles, pause for a moment or two.

Taking a Closer Look at Our Aspirations

When the time feels right, take a couple of deep breaths. Now call your full name out as loudly and as fully as you are able. The more strength and conviction you can give to your name the better. As you call out your name slowly you are likely to find that you pronounce your name slightly differently as you emphasise each syllable. This does not matter.

As you call out your name, feel the energy that is present in the words that name you. Observe your response to this. Then, when you are ready, call out your name again. Note the energy you are now experiencing, and again observe your response. When the moment feels right, call out your name once more, again noting the energy that is present in your name and your response to this.

Take a moment now to rest in the silence, and to absorb all that you have experienced. As you do so, pause to honour the uniqueness of who you are. Now, as you remain in this energy you might like to offer up this short prayer:

'O, Great Spirit, thank you for the gift of my life and for all the potential that it holds. As I seek to embrace each moment, help me to stand in the centre of who I am, so that I might live more fully. I ask that you will guide and protect me, and that you will bless all that I seek to do. And may each and every day of my life be a celebration of all that is sacred within and around me.'

Now, as you get ready to move on, may you take with you this new sense of who you are in your entirety. And when you are able, perhaps you might like to continue to chant your name now and again, with all the sacred purpose that you would bring to a mantra, so that you may continue to hold firm to who you really are.

1. Injecting Loving-Kindness into All That We Do

*Through an ever-increasing love in the heart
you will grow wise.*
WHITE EAGLE

IN A WORLD THAT IS SAFE THERE IS RESPECT

There is nothing our planet needs more than loving-kindness, than the ability to tread with grace through the many situations life presents us, so that always we treat our selves and others with great care. Loving-kindness is the expression of profound love performed lightly. It is an attribute we give little value to, and yet there are immense benefits for us all when we are able to be kind.

For too long we have been socialised to take care of our selves and to expect others to do the same. In business we are told that there are only the quick and the dead, and while we talk about win–win solutions, increasingly we are expected to win at any or all costs. We play with each other's lives as if we were playing a game, not realising that every time we do put someone down, something inside of us dies. By forsaking our compassion and decency, we lower our personal vibrations, allow our sense of connectedness to fade and become lesser human beings.

When we learn to meet others where they are at and to honour their life's journey, however flawed, we are mindful that they also carry within them that which is sacred. Where there is this level of respect in relationships, everyone feels safe and appreciated – safe to be who they are, regardless of their colour or creed or anything else we allow to divide us. And so when we are kind to others we enable them to touch the sacred beauty and tenderness of life.

Learning to love our selves

Loving-kindness is not so much about being nice as it is about learning to locate the Light of divine goodness within, and sharing this with others. If we are serious about embracing this path, then we must begin with our selves. While we frequently complain about the ways others treat us, often they are nowhere near as unforgiving as we are towards our selves. We only have to listen to the internal dialogue that unfolds when we have made a mistake to get a sense of this. And so as we seek to make loving-kindness part of our lives, we need to learn to relax a bit and to stop punishing our selves every time things don't go the way we had hoped.

We need to give our selves permission to do what we love. So often we postpone our opportunities for happiness, because we're too busy or too tired, or because we don't think the time is right, not realising how easily loving-kindness can propel us into a whole new space.

To be kind to our selves we need to be clear that we are worthy of good things. This means valuing our selves enough to have some time out. It might be as simple as taking the long way home from work because it's more scenic, or saying no to an evening out because we desperately need a night at home alone. Or we might decide to escape to the movies or take time to walk in a nearby park. This is not about being self-indulgent so much as carving out a little time in the day to do something that makes us feel good.

These are simple gestures that make a difference, because when we allow our selves moments of happiness we nurture every part of our being, and it is easier for us to feel more worthwhile. In feeling worthwhile, we are then able to help others do likewise.

Enhancing our inner Light

Making a commitment to our selves means doing those things that make our souls sing, that connect us with our sacred essence. Each one of us is made of Light, and whenever we do something, however humble, to enhance the Light in our selves or another, again we are advancing our own enlightenment.

The more we inject Light into our lives, the more readily we attain lasting peace and happiness. Sometimes we fear we have nothing to give, not realising that the path of loving-kindness is not so much about striving to do this or say that as it is about opening up to the Sacred and allowing its love to flow into us and through us. When we are able to do this, then our cup will run over, because we will be more at one with those around us.

Embracing the abundance of the universe

Sometimes we fail to be kind and generous because we fear there might not be enough love to go round, or we don't believe it is worth our effort. When we think like this, it is a sure sign that our world view has shrunk and that the possibilities for our lives have diminished also. When, however, we find the room in our hearts to be kind, then we are affirming that there are enough resources and enough love and hope for every one of us. And what we think, we draw to us.

How best to give

Today the whole issue of giving and receiving has become a complex one. We live in a world of flamboyant, often empty, gestures, where giving can get tangled up with appearances. Yet as we grow in wisdom and love, we are able to move beyond the many expectations that are not helpful to us, to a realisation that what matters most is that we come from a place of authenticity in all we say and do.

Loving-kindness does stretch our capacity to give and receive. Most of us are better at one side of the equation than the other. What loving-kindness does is nudge us forward until we are equally at home with giving as with receiving, because both are essential to our life experience. When we partake of kindness we are moved beyond our own narrow concerns and are inspired to embrace the world around us without condition. When we allow others to express their kindness, we allow the Sacred within them to blossom.

A return to community

The practice of loving-kindness is not about adding several more items to our 'to do' list but about making loving gestures a habit. In times past people recognised their need of each other, and even though they had less, they willingly shared what resources they had. The elderly had help with their shopping, with maintaining their homes and their gardens. The sick and the bereaved had meals made for them. New parents received support from friends and neighbours. Few of us are saints and yet we too can start by stretching our attention beyond our selves, so that we are more aware of those around us. When we do, the most magical things can take place.

Some years ago I met Venero, an elderly gentleman who had left Italy years before with his young friend Vito. When the two young men arrived in their new homeland they worked hard to establish themselves. They remained close friends even when they married and had children. As the years passed they began to grow apart, until they hadn't spoken in almost twenty years. Then one day Venero seized the moment and rang his old friend. Vito's wife answered the phone. Although Vito was unwell, she assured Venero he was welcome to visit.

When Venero arrived at his friend's home he discovered Vito was dying, and within a week Vito had passed away. Venero was inconsolable. When he visited Vito's widow he confessed his shame at having allowed the years to slip past. 'You've got it all wrong,' Vito's widow assured him. 'For years Vito missed your friendship, but he did nothing about it. Seeing you again made him so happy. It helped him to die in peace.'

Finding the strength to support those who need us most

In a world that honours loving-kindness, we find the courage and the will to take others with us – not just the strong and the brave, but all those who rely on our decency and compassion to survive. Those communities and nations that are the most progressive care for the weak and honour the strong. And every time a society becomes greedy and self-satisfied, every time it ignores or preys on the helpless, it sows the seeds of its own destruction.

Our whole world is hungry. Some are hungry for food and

shelter, while others are hungry for love and recognition, for a true sense of meaning and worth. Yet if the life of each person on the planet was regularly touched by some act of loving-kindness there would be no hunger, because those who have plenty, whether it be food or love, would willingly see to the nurture of those who do not. How awesome then is our task?

Being there for others

Practising loving-kindness is about waking up to the people around us, about peering beneath the social niceties to see what is really needed. This might then mean that we make the effort to give someone a hug or a welcome cup of coffee. Or it might mean that we pray for someone by simply asking that they be blessed.

This might not seem to be significant but Dr Emoto, who has been researching the quality of water for many years, has discovered something extraordinary. He has taken thousands upon thousands of water samples and analysed them, including those from some of the most polluted waterways on the planet. Not surprisingly the polluted water shows clear evidence of its contamination. When, however, that same water has been blessed, its essential nature is transformed and there are beautiful crystalline shapes present in the water at a microscopic level that weren't there previously. So even when we bless someone with a hug or a prayer, make no mistake, this is a highly meaningful act.

It is easy to assume we can't do a great deal because we are just one person, when in fact we can sometimes achieve remarkable things without even trying. Some time ago a friend was devastated by a documentary on the orphans in Rumania. Although she led a busy life farming in a fairly remote location, she knew she had to do something to help these poor children. When she sat down and thought about it she realised she could knit jumpers and blanket squares, and could encourage her close friends to do the same. Each friend she approached went on to contact several more friends, until a few months later literally hundreds of jumpers and blankets had been made. No one could have achieved this by themselves, but collectively these women achieved something extraordinary.

When we find the room in our hearts to reach out to others, we encourage them to participate in the greater good, thus enhancing the Light in the world. Then we discover that whatever gesture we perform will have an extraordinary sense of rightness about it for everyone involved.

This was very much the case for an Irish friend who was on a working holiday a long way from home. As Christmas approached, her thoughts turned to her friends and family. Then as she went to leave on Christmas Eve, someone she hardly knew pressed a small present into her hand, explaining they had spent time in Ireland years before, and had been overwhelmed by the kindness they had received. This tiny gift was their way of returning some of that kindness. This humble gesture touched my friend deeply, and who is to say that such a simple gesture won't be repeated somewhere else in the world at some future time?

Discovering what we are made of

We can only discover our own inner strength when we *practise* the values we seek to embody. It is much easier to be loving when life is going well. When times are hard, loving-kindness requires us to be more creative. It nudges us forward, encouraging us to push back our boundaries so that we can discover the strength we have within us. And when we have the courage to follow its promptings, we learn how to maintain a gracious spirit even when our physical, mental or emotional resources are thin.

When we are able to support and encourage others, and continue to hold a good space for them, even when we feel low, then we will find this goodness will return to us many times over, warming our lives when we need it most. At one stage a good friend Mae, who was always doing kind things for others, was feeling very down. She had been working hard and even though she was a naturally optimisitic person, she had started to feel apprehensive about the future. Mae remembers hanging out the washing late one night and asking for some guidance as to what lay ahead. The following day she had a meeting for work with someone she had never met before. At the end of their discussions the person paused, then told Mae she had an angelic message for her, and proceeded to address every concern Mae had about the future.

The magic of loving-kindness is that it reaches beyond all our preconceptions of how life should unfold and reaches those places within us that are crying out for nurture. Loving-kindness seeks out our wounds and heals them with the Light and Love we so desperately need. Then we come to understand that loving-kindness is simply another form of healing, which reaches deep inside and mends what needs mending.

A prayer to help us be kind

'O, Great Spirit, life can be so exacting that sometimes it is hard to be kind. Help me to move beyond my own weariness and despair, so that I too can practise loving-kindness and thus illuminate my life and the lives of those around me. Help me also to understand that true kindness is not weakness. True kindness is for those of us who dare to be strong,

Injecting Loving-kindness

who have the courage to reach out soul to soul so that we can allow beauty and goodness and truth to flow through us and into the world around us. Help me to see for myself that there is enough love for everyone and that whatever I give out will return to me many times over, blessing me when I need it most.'

DISCOVERING OUR OWN SACRED SPACE

FINDING OUR SACRED SPACE
The choice to incarnate at this time is an immense one, because we have chosen to take on human form at one of the most momentous times in the history of human consciousness. This is a great privilege, but it can be a great challenge also. And so as we seek to embrace our human adventure it is important for us to remember that in amongst all we strive for we need to nurture our selves – mind, body and spirit.

We can only do this when we are aware of the people and environments and lifestyles that sustain us and those that do not. When our bodies are stressed and sluggish and our minds full of chatter, then there's little room for anything else. When, however, we are in tune, we are able to begin to discover all wisdom and in-sight available to us.

One of the best ways to nurture our selves is to find those special places nearby where we can be at one with our selves. I call these places sacred, because they help align us with the sacred presence in all things.

There is a beautiful beach ringed by ancient trees with spectacular twisted trunks I visit regularly, and it is here amid the solid splendour of the trees and the sea and the sky where I reflect. It is here I get many of my best ideas, and where I am most aware of my connection with all living things.

Given the choice between this and a hundred and one other activities, I would choose this place every time, because here among the quiet and the beauty the mental chatter ceases and my mind clears. Here my whole being comes back into balance.

I recently learned that my sacred place was called the healing place by our indigenous peoples. How wonderful is that! Part of me wasn't surprised to hear this, because regardless of where we live, when we listen to our inner voice we will find the space that is right for us.

These spaces are important to us, because they take us deep inside, enabling us to see how our inner and outer worlds are connected. Then we discover that whatever work we do on our selves, however seemingly insignificant, will transform the way we operate within the world. I am never the same person returning home as the one who set out. The one who returns is always a little wiser and clearer, and more rested as well.

Seeking meaningful solitude

Do you know a sacred space already or is it yours to discover? Be assured that there is a special space awaiting you, and when you make the effort to spend time there you will be richly rewarded.

Access to these kinds of places can be life-changing, but only when we are committed to putting aside time to be there. We can only carve out time for our selves when we plan our quiet times with as much energy as we give to everything else in our lives. Then, having made these plans, it is up to us to honour them.

The Bible suggests we work six days, then rest on the seventh day. This possibility was never about being damned if we didn't sit still, but about balancing our times of action with non-action, so that we have time out to sit by a river or to walk through a forest and be sustained by these soul-nurturing experiences.

While we might not be able to put aside a whole day a week for rest, or at least not in a single block of time, we can find the time and space to contemplate, to be inspired. And when we can find somewhere to retreat to whenever we need to be alone, then we are blessed indeed.

Sacred journeying

Sometimes the opportunity for a brief respite in our week is all we need to maintain our sense of balance, but there are times when we need to undertake a longer journey of body and soul. These journeys were once known as pilgrimages, and the peoples undertaking them understood their value and purpose. At least once in their lives they would try to undertake a pilgrimage in the expectation that a level of grace and illumination would follow. Sometimes people would travel alone and sometimes in groups. They would set off with the clear desire to know more of themselves and to feel the gentle hand of the Great Spirit on their lives. Often they would travel far and for a considerable time, but it was the opportunity to leave behind the everyday world with all its distractions and responsibilities that was central.

Most of us don't have the leisure to spend weeks or months away from our homes and jobs, but still we can immerse ourselves in the depth of this kind of experience and see where it takes us. When we are ready for a soul journey we will know it as clearly as we know our own name. The call might be sparked by something we read or by a sudden inspiration. The way it calls us is inconsequential – what matters is that we recognise the signs and have the courage to respond to them.

Discovering Our Own Sacred Space

For me the call came in a dream. I was instructed to embark on a quest through the desert. In my dream I then made my way deep into the desert, until I could go no further, and as the heat intensified my life slipped slowly away. I watched on, unafraid, as the desert sands covered me. The whole experience had such a strong sense of rightness that there seemed no reason to be sad or afraid. I was aware I had become one with the vast sands, and with much more besides. Then without warning I was an eagle, dipping and swirling through a cloudless sky, and my whole being soared to see this.

I had no idea what my dream meant, other than it was an important one. I knew it was a message about spiritual metamorphosis, and so I began to work more intensely on myself. Months passed and still the dream remained, until I had the opportunity to go with my husband to the great Southwestern Desert of the United States – to Anasazi country. Apart from reading up a little about the places we would visit, I made no plans, as I felt that we were being asked to simply open our selves up to the experience.

From the moment we headed out into the desert we had a strong sense of coming home. Each day as we travelled deeper into the beauty and power of this place, everything that was unimportant began to drop away. I had always feared barren landscapes – I feared their stark unyielding qualities and the fact there was no place to hide. And yet once we were there my fear evaporated. There are many places on Earth where one can feel the sacred presence of the Great Spirit and the connectedness to all living things, but there are few places that hold this much clarity and aliveness.

The day we arrived at Monument Valley I was thunderstruck, because this was the landscape of my dream. In no time our

Navajo guide had packed us into his jeep, and we were off bouncing along a dirt track out into the heart of the valley. We had only been going a short while when he braked, swung round in his seat and fixed me with his dark eyes, declaring that I had not come to see the scenery.

I told him I had had a dream and he simply nodded as we travelled on under the midday sun. Here and there our guide stopped to share his world with us. Then he took us inside a cave in one of their cliffs and sang the ancient songs of his people. My heart cracked open at the sacred beauty and I wept with deep joy as the precious time slipped away.

We were silent as we drove away. Now at last I had experienced the transformative power of the wilderness in full. So charged was this time with wisdom that this experience felt as essential to me as my own flesh and blood. We returned home and a few weeks later a friend arrived from London with a CD of sacred music, on which was one of the songs our guide had sung to us on our unforgettable day in Monument Valley. Even now the power of that experience reaches out to us, and the sheer expanse and majesty of the landscape is indelibly etched on our souls.

MAKING THE MOST OF OUR SOUL JOURNEY
When we consider journeys such as these, what matters is that we choose a place that we suspect can touch our soul – where the inner and outer worlds can meet and where we can be transformed in some way. Then, once we have reached our sacred destination, if we allow each moment to unfold as it happens and look deeply at the world around us, we will begin to experience the wonder and beauty and intense sacredness of life at a whole new level. We will glimpse at what it is like to experience the

profound oneness of all beings. When we are able to make this level of connection, it is ours for life, enabling us to inject much-needed purpose into all that we do.

Preparing for our soul journey

When we are planning a journey of body and spirit we stand on the brink of a great adventure, and even if the location isn't already apparent to us, it doesn't matter. There are many possibilities available and inspiration is sure to follow. It does need to be somewhere that is relatively untouched by civilisation, that will lift us out of the familiar, so that we can commune with the Sacred.

Once the location is chosen, then the more of our everyday lives and comforts we can leave behind the better. We must be free to embrace all those things we had forgotten about, as we allow the sun to warm our skin and the rain to fall gently upon us. We then experience the elation of eating because we are hungry, and not simply because we are bored or stressed. We appreciate our food, not because it has been cooked by a well-known chef, but because we recognise the profound blessing that even the most basic meal brings. And, because we have the time, we are able to consciously eat our food, to taste each mouthful and give thanks for it.

Our sacred journey is a practical journey also

A true journey of the soul is not so much about finding answers to every question we have up our sleeves as it is about discovering where the source of our unfailing wisdom lies. It is not so much about discovering our soul mate as it is about coming home to that sacred place inside, where we belong and where all our needs can be met. These gifts are profound, because they take us far beyond the instant solutions we so often seek. When we understand these things, we finally know we are well on our way to locating our true selves.

Choosing our locations and companions with care

As these times are precious it is far better to travel by our selves and risk feeling alone now and again than to invite others along who do not share our vision. We need also to ensure that there is sufficient time to be at one with an experience, and so in looking at our itinerary it is better to soak up the benefits of one or two places than it is to experience anything and everything in sight.

Letting go of our preconceptions

As we find our selves wondering what may or may not unfold, it is essential we abandon all expectations. Sometimes when we set off on these journeys it is easy to lose the magic of the moment by seeking signs and wonders. The Great Spirit can only reach us when we are receptive, so we need to relax into our journey to experience all that is around us. It is only as we slow down that we are able to still the chatter and the notions that chase around in our heads. Often we will have no idea of the extent of the healing or teaching that is taking place until we return home.

Easing our selves back into everyday life

One of the hardest parts of undertaking a soul journey can be the return home, unless we handle our re-entry with care. When we have had the great joy and illumination of the mountain-top experiences, often, mistakenly, we are reluctant to leave them behind. We fear that once we depart they will be lost to us, when in fact the mountain-top experiences are given to us to sustain and nurture us, so that we are then able to transform our everyday lives into something far more meaningful.

On our return we are likely to be re-entering the denser energies of towns and cities, so we need to be aware that from an energetic perspective our homecoming might be challenging. That said the more in tune we are with the Sacred, the less our homecoming will affect us. The benefits we have gained will remain with us. We will also discover that much of what pre-occupied us no longer holds our attention.

The more gently we can ease our selves back into daily life, the better the transition will be. And so the less social contact we have over the first couple of weeks, other than returning to work and attending to our families, the better. This enables us to continue to savour the depth of in-sight and healing we have received.

GIVING THANKS FOR ALL WE HAVE GAINED

Once we are back it is important that we make time to give thanks for our many blessings. It helps to find a special time and place to give thanks. First we can give thanks to the Great Spirit – to the great guiding influence in our lives – and then we can name all the people and places that have helped us along the way, including those who kept things going while we were gone. We can then ask that they be blessed a hundred times over.

This done, it is then time for us to embrace the everyday once more. This can be a heady time, as we begin to experience the new sense of vision and purpose our soul journey has brought us. Yet always we must ensure our feet are firmly on the ground, so that we don't seek to dismiss others because they are not on our wavelength. Instead as we harness our in-sight we are now able to look more deeply at those around us and see them more completely. We might well see that they have not been as fortunate in their life's journey as we have. And in seeing this we are then able to treat them with more love and respect, aware that by so doing we are filling their lives with Light and hope. When we are able to conduct our selves in this way, we allow others to benefit from all that we have been given as well.

Honouring our wise ones
Sacred space is to be found not only in places but in the people who delight us body and soul. The more attuned we are to those of like energy, the more they will appear in our lives. Some years ago I was told I would meet my tribe. This wasn't a cluster of people close by, but a network of like-minded people unknown to each other around the planet. Since that time many remarkable souls have appeared in my life, blessing me with their extraordinary love and unique vision. These I now recognise as my wise ones – souls who have travelled far and who have learnt a great deal. These Light-bearers are truly wonderful friends, and while they are not all elderly in Earth years, they are without doubt old souls.

Most do not even live in the same city. Some don't even live in my part of the globe, and some I have never met in the flesh. Often we might not connect for months, but whenever we do the moments we share are moments out of time. They come into my life when they are least expected. They light my path and hopefully I do theirs.

We all have wise ones at different times in our lives. And so even if there doesn't appear to be anyone there for you at present, there will be. Our wise ones turn up when we are ready to hear what they have to say. Frequently they appear to be so ordinary that we do not always recognise them for who they really are, until they surprise us with something that is truly inspired, and then we can appreciate just how extraordinary they are.

A prayer to help us find the Sacred in the people and places around us

'O, Great Spirit, help me to find those places nearby that can provide me with the sacred space I need to replenish mind, body and soul. And in finding these spaces, help me to open up to all the positive energies available to me there. Help me also to find those who are wise and true, so that I too might join the network of Light that encircles our planet.'

Sacred Practices to Enhance Our Lives

Enhancing the Light

As most of us no longer take part in any formal religious observances, we assume we can do without them altogether, not realising how central sacred practices and teachings are to sustaining us body and soul. Sacred practice enhances the Light within and around us, and gives us the direction and in-sight we need to gain enlightenment. The choice to take up our sacred practices is ours alone – if we choose to pass on them we won't be damned, but it will be harder for us to move forward.

Sacred practice has much to offer, but it does require our participation and commitment. Should we take up sacred practice our lives will undoubtedly change. Still there will be days when life flows, and days when it doesn't and we are tempted not to bother. Yet if we don't do our practice, we can't benefit from it.

The practice of meditation

One of the cornerstones of sacred practice is daily meditation, because it grounds our lives in the Divine Light within us. And once we are able to enjoy this daily connection with our divinity, it is easier for us to connect with the sacred mystery and beauty of life wherever we might be.

The benefits of meditation are many. On a physical level it clears the mind and slows the metabolism. It also broadens our horizons, enabling us to take a more panoramic view of our lives. It is invaluable for problem-solving, and for enhancing our creativity as well. Not only does it inject our days with a tangible sense of peace and wellbeing, it allows us to live within a higher energy, enabling us to then become increasingly aware of energies that are or are not good for us.

All we need is twenty minutes a day. At first this might seem a stretch, but once we experience the benefits for our selves it will become an invaluable part of our everyday lives. For years I have travelled, working long and often irregular hours, and yet even when it meant getting up really early I continued to meditate, because meditation makes such a difference to my day. On the rare days I don't meditate I feel as if I haven't had enough sleep.

Getting the most out of meditation

An excellent time to meditate is first thing in the morning. Before meditation it helps to spend a moment or two outside or by an open window, so that we can absorb the nuances of the new day. Whenever we meditate it is advisable to do so before meals, and to ensure that wherever we are meditating is not overheated, otherwise we are likely to drift off to sleep. We should try to have a door or window open for fresh air, if possible.

If morning meditation isn't possible, we need to choose another time of day when we are likely to feel receptive – early evening is often an excellent time for this. Absolute quiet is critical. It is important to remember to take the phone off its cradle, to put pets out of the way, and to find somewhere comfortable to settle down. It helps to meditate in the same place each day, so that over time this special space in our home gathers sacred energies around it. This doesn't mean that we can't use this space for other purposes, but that as we settle down to meditate, this routine helps us draw our attention within. Some people also find it helpful to wear a shawl during meditation. Again this can help us enter meditation more easily, because the shawl will become imbued with the lighter energy we experience during meditation.

It is useful to have a book of inspirational quotes or a sacred text to hand. I always start meditation by reading a random passage out of the book by White Eagle, *The Quiet Mind*. Even though I have read some segments a hundred times or more, each time I do so another layer of meaning is revealed to me. Why not find your own book of in-sights to read from each day?

A meditation for those with busy lives

There are many different forms of meditation. The following one is excellent for those with busy lives, because it takes us to a deep place without effort and it can be done anywhere quiet.

Sitting comfortably, with your eyes closed, your back straight, your feet planted firmly on the floor and your hands in your lap, become aware of your breathing. Then as you breathe slowly in and out offer up this brief prayer:

'May the words of my mouth and the meditation of my heart be acceptable in Thy sight, O, Great Spirit.'

As you follow your breath in and out, allow your attention to come into the room. Allow any sounds or thoughts to drift past as you breathe slowly in and out. Now, as you bring your attention into your body, let your shoulders drop and your stomach soften. Then, as you continue to breathe slowly in and out, allow any tensions to dissolve. It is time now to relax and invite the Sacred into this moment.

As you continue to breathe slowly in and out, feel every part of your being becoming still. Experience the deep calm that comes with this stillness. If any thoughts arise, observe them, then let them go. With each inward-breath allow yourself to go deeper into the moment. Whenever you feel yourself becoming distracted, simply bring your attention back to your breath as you continue to breathe in and out, in and out, in and out . . .

Then, when it is time to emerge from meditation, slowly bring your attention back into your body. Taking deeper, fuller breaths, return to the present moment. Before you open your eyes, bow your head in a silent gesture of thanks.

Then, as you open your eyes, allow your attention to return to the room. Savour this moment as you take in the wonder of this day and of your life. How blessed you are, are you not? As you rest in the beautiful energy of your meditation you might then like to offer up this prayer as you visualise your whole being radiating with Light:

'I choose this day to be surrounded by the energy of the Great White Light. May it surround and suffuse and protect every part of me, and may it inform all that I do, think and say. Thank you, O Great Spirit, for this day of my life. May it be a blessing to myself and to all I meet. And now as I enter this new day may the Light of the Sacred go before me, guiding, uplifting and sustaining me in all aspects of my life.'

Evaluating our meditation

Often we place many expectations on our selves. We want to be immediately perfect at whatever we are doing, but spiritual progress is more fluid. We are often undergoing spiritual growth on several levels at once, and so when we meditate it is best simply to embrace the experience. On the days we can't still the mental chatter during meditation, there is no need to become disheartened – all we need do is simply observe our thoughts and let them pass.

Then as we re-enter our day, we can take a moment to note the thoughts concerned, knowing that whatever was distracting us is taking a great deal of our life energy right now. We are then able to recognise that these same thoughts are diminishing our contact with the Divine.

At such times, it helps to offer up a silent prayer to the Great Spirit, admitting our concerns and asking for help to let them go. That done, forget them. And if they return, simply dismiss them. Remember we are in charge of our destiny, and our thoughts create our destiny.

The cumulative effects of meditation

Meditation is a journey back to our true self, to that state of perfect happiness, in-sight and love. As time goes by not only will we carry this meditative calm with us into everyday life, we will reach the point where every waking moment is lived within this profound meditative energy. And so the more commitment we have to our meditation, the more we will benefit from it.

The practice of observation

We can further assist our enlightening process by learning the sacred practice of observation. We do this by consciously stepping back from the intensity of the moment and observing our selves and others objectively as we go about our everyday lives. When we are able to do this successfully, it is as if we are watching our lives on video. Not only are we able to observe others more closely, we can see our selves in a new light as well. We then start to see into our heart and our motives, into our strengths and insecurities, and into the hearts of those around us.

Making regular use of this practice helps us become aware of what is really going on in our lives. We begin to notice the tone of voice we use, the ways we do and don't respond, and what is in need of our attention. We might then discover we have a tendency not to listen to what others are saying because we are so eager to talk. We might even realise that the person who always seemed so rude and evasive has no self-confidence, and that when we react to them we make them feel even less secure.

This ability to see clearly is invaluable, because life is no longer such a mystery or a challenge. Then, even when in volatile situations, we are able to distance our selves from all the emotion and find a positive outcome for all concerned.

The practice of gratitude

Along with the practice of observation is that of gratitude. It is easy to become so weighed down with the business of living that we forget we are greatly blessed. Already we have access to sufficient food and shelter and freedom of speech and so much more. When we are able to move beyond those things which get us down and recognise all we have to be thankful for, then life takes on a different quality. Our lives feel more expansive, and even the smallest gesture becomes an opportunity for a deep and sustained sense of joy.

When we talk of the sacred practice of gratitude we are

describing the ability to perceive the world the way we did when we were children. Back then each day was a new chapter. We were able to delight in everything that came our way, and so it was that life would reveal its magic to us.

Of course there are times when life stretches us, or when everything everyone else is doing appears to be more important or more interesting. This is the perfect time to invite the practice of gratitude back into our lives, and to rediscover the profound possibilities available to us in this moment.

While shopping we can give thanks for having enough clothes to wear and enough food to eat. As we go to sleep at night we can then give thanks for a clean bed and for a roof over our heads. When we are able to appreciate even the most basic aspects of our lives, we enhance the Sacred in everything we do. We then discover what the wise have always known – that concealed within the seemingly ordinary experiences of life is the very presence of God.

Learning to take good care of our bodies

As we become increasingly aware of the myriad energies we encounter daily, we start to care about the environment we live in. Familiarity with those energies that enhance our sacred essence and those that do not then inspires us to take note of our lifestyles and of the effects that various kinds of food and drink have on us. Some years ago it became apparent I would feel better if I no longer drank alcohol or ate meat. When I gave up these things I began to experience far greater clarity and lightness of being, and far from feeling I was missing out I began to experience a greater sense of freedom than before. This is not everyone's path, but we do need to take note of our own inner guidance.

When we talk of giving up something it is easy to assume we are being deprived in some way. In the realms of the Sacred, however, it is our very ability to let go of those things we don't need that enables us to travel lighter and further than would have otherwise been the case.

Blessing the close of our day

At the end of the day, along with our natural weariness comes the opportunity to contemplate all that has happened to us. This is the time when again we can consciously reconnect with the Divine and give thanks for our life and all we have received. We can also use this time to ask for assistance for those things we need help with. If there is time, it helps to meditate at the end of the day as well.

Then each night as we close our eyes we can ask that we be bathed in Light and that the Great Spirit protect us while we slumber. This is important, because rarely do we remain in our bodies while sleeping. I first became aware of this when an uncle of mine who lived on the other side of the world almost died from heart problems. For a couple of days his life hung in the balance. I didn't know he was sick until some weeks later when he contacted me to tell me that I had watched over him while he was unconscious. At the time I was shaken by what he said, but over the years I have come to understand a great deal more of what is possible during sleep.

Making the most of our sleep

In a peaceful few moments before sleep, read a speech or some information you need to remember the following day. Read it slowly and ask that you may be able to continue to work with this material while you're asleep. Then, before you finally drift off to sleep, let go of the material in your mind – this is critical. Whenever I have done this, the results have been excellent. This doesn't mean we don't have to do the groundwork during our waking lives, but that we get the chance for extra rehearsals or inspiration while we sleep. Why not try this? You will be amazed at the outcome.

In accordance with the laws of the universe, as we receive so we should give out, and so we can also ask that our inner Light be of solace or healing to others while we sleep. This isn't hard to do. Before we sleep we can request to help people we know, or to assist those in one of the world's many trouble spots. If there is one good reason for glancing at the daily papers or watching the evening news, it is to inform our selves of what is happening, so that we know where we might send our Light while we sleep. And always while we sleep we must ask for the protection and illumination of the Light.

As we attend to our sacred practice, we tend to that part of us that transcends time and space, that part of us that already knows all things. We are then able to tap into this deep wisdom and consciously make it our own.

A prayer to assist us with our sacred practices
'O, Great Spirit, as I consider the possibilities for my life, help me to find the sacred practices that are most appropriate for me right now, so that each and every day I am enhancing the Light within and around me, and thus making progress on my journey towards lightness of being.'

WHO AM I?

*We were born to make manifest the glory of God within us.
It's not just in some of us; it's in everyone.
And as we let our own light shine,
we unconsciously give other people permission to do the same.*
AUTHOR UNKNOWN

EMBRACING THE FREEDOM AVAILABLE TO US

If we are spiritual beings having a human experience, what exactly does this mean? Who are we really? If we ignore the fact that we are male or female, young or old, black or white, what remains? What is that part of us that stretches beyond the limitations of our minds and bodies? What part of us existed before this time and will continue long after we have departed this life?

Regardless of the specifics of culture, education or religion, humankind has always enjoyed a sense of the Divine through personal revelation and spiritual teachings. Yet over time this connection with the numinous has faded to the point that many of us have little or no sense of our sacred potential.

The present time is one of the most remarkable periods of history. In a few short years some of the most formidable religious structures have crumbled, and we are now able to enjoy a spiritual freedom rarely experienced before. Now many of the great teachings are readily available, allowing us to see more clearly the awesome nature of all we carry within us.

Discovering our true selves

How then can we realise our potential? Ramana Maharshi, one of India's most exquisite spiritual teachers, taught that the only question we need ask our selves is 'Who Am I?' This, he declared, is the key to becoming enlightened. Details of this can be found in the book *Ramana Maharshi and the Path of Self-Knowledge* by Arthur Osborne.

When we ask 'Who Am I?', the question appears simple, and in truth it is, because it reaches to the heart of who we are. Yet when we try to formulate an answer, our certainty fades. So defined are we by our background that at first it is hard for us to have any sense of our selves beyond our labels. Often we hide behind these labels believing they give us meaning and credibility.

Ramana Maharshi exhorted us to follow this enquiry each and every day and for good reason – when we ask 'Who Am I?' we are seeking that which we *already* are. And when finally we arrive at the answer, we discover the awesome nature of human life in all its dimensions.

Who are we really?

When we ask our selves 'Who Am I?', this is not an attempt to negate everything we have done, but an attempt to move beyond things that are familiar so we can discover whole aspects of our selves we had no idea existed. The answer to this profound question is not something we arrive at in a week or a month – it is a lifelong question to be explored in moments of silence, as well as in moments of exhaustion and confusion. Each time we are genuine about asking our selves this question, in-sight will follow.

When we are young we are fortunate, because there is little that separates us from our divine essence. Then as we begin to take our place in the world our sense of our sacred self tends to slip away. Increasingly our life's energy is spent in securing our place in life – in work, in establishing a home and a family. As the years slip by there are more and more labels, until we have no real sense of who we are. We often fear that without the labels our lives lack meaning. Yet it is not the abandonment of our labels we need to worry about so much as our increasing dependency on these things to give our lives meaning.

Our search for that part of us that exists within and beyond the limits of time and space is like the game of pass the parcel we played as children. Each time the parcel landed in our lap we would tear eagerly at the paper in the hope that the next wrapping was the last, only to find there were many more layers to remove before we discovered what was concealed within the parcel. On our journey back to our true selves, slowly and painstakingly we need to peel back the layers of identity we have acquired, so that we can see what lies beneath. The more layers we uncover, the more exhilarating our journey becomes.

Seeing our ego for what it is

When we start to ask our selves 'Who Am I?', we begin to discover all those things we are not. We start to recognise the ever-present voice of our ego that claims far more ownership of our lives than it has the right to. We begin to see how it drives us to do this or think that. We then recognise the 'I' that clings to the corner office or to the brand-new car. The 'I' that leads us to believe we are indispensable, that prompts us to go for the next promotion and the next, not because it feeds our soul but just so that others will take note, is the 'I' of the ego. Once we can recognise just how insidious our ego can be, we begin to see our life in all its vanity and fragility. We then see all the times we sell our selves and others short. Knowing this we are then in a position to move beyond this unsatisfactory way of living.

Life beyond ego

Once we are able to see our lives as they are, we are able to begin to let go of all that our ego clings to. By turning our attention away from the purely material aspects of life, we can stop becoming caught up in family dramas, in office politics, or in the need to prove our selves at the expense of others. Instead we start to get a life beyond these things. We find our selves being able to appreciate aspects of our everyday lives in ways we had never thought possible.

No longer do we waste time worrying about our weight, our wardrobe or our wrinkles. Even when our bodies begin to age we do not feel diminished, because we realise our bodies are home to our spirit. And because we are no longer bound by our physical selves, we are then more motivated to embrace and nurture them.

We realise that what matters most is not how we describe our selves, but how we live and what we have learned. And the more we get to know our true selves, the more we are able to honour those around us as spiritual beings as well. No longer are they merely the accountant or the next-door neighbour, but fellow journeyers on an extraordinary quest. And as we embrace the Sacred in others, we discover that within us which soars to see a breathtaking sunset, that has the courage to reach out to the sick, the hungry or the abused.

As we make time to journey deep within and to make sense of our rich inner world, so our understanding of the outer world is transformed. We realise we are the vast blue of the sky and we are the dying soldier as much as we are those who work hard to bring peace, because we are in all living things and they are all in us.

A prayer to help us discover who we really are

'O, Great Spirit, as I seek to discover the awesome nature of my true self, help me to shed all those things I am not. Help me to see I AM more than flesh and blood, more than what is happening at present, so that I can begin to experience for myself the limitless nature of my divine self. As I journey on help me to move beyond the I of my ego, to the I deep within that is already one with all things.'

On Guidance

SEEKING THINGS THAT HAVE GENUINE DEPTH
Along our life's path we encounter many things that seem so innocuous we don't even give them a second thought, because we are so busy and so stressed most of the time. While this might be convenient we cannot afford to simply drift along in life. Our life's quest is a journey through the many veils of illusion, and so we need to remain alert to all that is around us so that we can discern the difference between those things that *seem* substantial and those that really are of substance.

When we can recognise the things that are real, as opposed to those things that appear real, our path will be smoother. This means learning to distinguish between things that are seemingly attractive and authoritative and things that do genuinely broaden our vision and make our souls sing.

LEARNING TO RECOGNISE OUR INNER VOICE
Just as we seek to discern those things that are real from those that are not in the external world, so too we must exercise the same discernment within. There are many voices that compete for our attention, but there is only one voice that will not fail

us, our inner voice. This is the voice that speaks to us in the moments of silence, that moves us to the very depths of our being. This is the all-wise voice of the Sacred that gives us hope and direction, that smooths our path and calms us when we are feeling weary or uncertain.

If we wish to benefit from our inner voice, we need to give ourselves the silence and space we need to appreciate its guidance. Then when we listen we must allow our inner voice to tell us those things we long to hear, as well as those we do not. There is little point in seeking life's wisdom if we are going to be selective about what we take note of – even if we don't understand the full importance of what is being suggested to us, the absolute benefit of this guidance will become apparent in time. Whatever the guidance we receive will be for our highest good, and often the outcome will surpass anything we could hope for.

KNOWING WHEN TO ACT AND WHEN TO REMAIN STILL

Sacred guidance is also about perfect timing. Sometimes we might have a project or idea we want to move on, yet if our inner guidance suggests otherwise, again we need to listen. The project or idea could be inappropriate for us, or the timing might not be right. If we forge ahead we might jeopardise something that would have been ideal further down the track. Similarly our inner guidance could be prompting us forward with what seems like undue haste, because now is the time to act.

GETTING THE GUIDANCE WE NEED

The guidance we receive won't always come from our inner voice. Sometimes it will be sparked by a chance conversation or by a sudden good idea. Again we can only recognise these promptings when we have the space in our lives to invite these things in. Sometimes these promptings will be genuine, and sometimes they will be the voice of our ego, and so we need to consult our inner voice to see the truth of the situation. Learning to act in accordance with our inner voice is not about seeing our selves as some sort of oracle, but about relying on that sacred part within us where true in-sight resides.

We can only develop a relationship with our inner guidance when we are prepared to let go a little and allow the wider spectrum of life's possibilities to be made apparent to us. This can be scary at first – so used are we to being in control that it can be hard to allow our selves to be more intuitive. Yet when we can summon the courage to listen to our inner voice and have the foresight to follow its guidance, our lives will be far more joyous because we will no longer feel adrift on our quest. And the more we experience the support of the universe, the more we are willing to make it part of our lives.

Our inner guidance is not merely for spiritual progress, it is often highly practical guidance as well. Good friends were on a trip to South America when they had a strong feeling they should change their flights and stay where they were another day. It wasn't a practical decision to make, because bookings were tight at the time. Following their inner guidance they did change their flights, only to discover a few hours later that the plane they had been booked on crashed, killing all on board.

Sometimes we will be guided to take a different approach to an issue than is expected of us. This can be challenging, because it might require us to step outside our comfort zone. We might even find that those we love will try to persuade us to maintain the status quo. When this happens it is tempting to give in, simply to keep others happy. And so when we are in this dilemma, we need to ask our selves whether we are honouring our own divinity or whether we are merely indulging the fragilities and expectations of those around us. Be assured that whatever guidance we are given will not only be right for us, but for everyone else as well.

Understanding the psychic dimension

As we begin to make serious progress we might start to experience an elementary psychic ability. We might even discover we can read people and situations with startling accuracy, or future events might be revealed to us in occasional flashes. Whatever happens we must realise that ultimately our psychic ability has no more bearing on our spiritual attainment than it does on our ability to make a decent meal or to climb mountains.

The psychic realm is very tantalising and something the ego is drawn to, because these gifts have the capacity to make us feel special, to get us noticed. At the end of the day, however, we must recognise that the realm of the psychic is often the realm of delusion, within which many have become hopelessly lost. There are wonderful people who use their psychic abilities to heal body and spirit, but there are also those who use their gifts to seek fame and fortune.

Approaching psychic guidance with care

While access to psychic guidance might be helpful, we must also remember that a reading will only ever be as good as the vehicle, and no matter how impressive anyone is, they are not the Great Spirit. We need also to be aware that this is our precious life's quest we are dealing with, so if the person is more interested in running a business or being a psychic superstar, they are unlikely to be the ideal person to help guide us on our life's quest. Whoever we consult should be someone well able to focus on our soul journey, because this is the knowledge we need above all else.

Often we seek guidance when we are determined to make something happen in our lives. We decide that what we need to be happy is a new partner or a new job and so that is the clarity we seek, not realising that what we need most right now are ways to make our lives genuinely complete. This might well include a new job or a new partner, or it might mean we are about to get the chance to travel the world and meet new and interesting people because the new partner or job isn't there for us yet. If we continue to fixate on what we want, we might well get what we are after, but it mightn't be the ideal place or person to feed us body and soul.

I have a male friend who is desperate for the perfect relationship. He has sought so much psychic advice about where his dream woman might be that he is now even more desperate and confused. This is not the guidance that helps us move forward on our life's quest. True guidance is about allowing life to reveal what is best for us, not about being allowed to run riot in the tuck shop of life.

Keeping our feet on the ground

Even in our darkest moments there will be guidance for us. The danger comes, however, when we become so dependent on psychic manifestations or on readings that we are no longer able to think for our selves, let alone access the deep wisdom that lies within us. So distracted can we become with the realms beyond our own that everything around us can then appear to be a sign and a wonder. When this happens it is a sure sign we have lost the plot. Unless we are genuinely moved to the depths of our being by these experiences, and unless they speak directly to our own inner voice, we should disregard them altogether.

Those with strong psychic abilities hold great responsibilities.

Always we must go deeper with our own sacred practice, because we can't teach what we don't know. It is all too easy to have honed certain gifts, then become so comfortable with them that we cease to learn and to grow. And when our spiritual growth comes to a halt, we are hardly likely to inspire our selves let alone anyone else.

If we do not retain our commitment to our sacred path, not only do we forget that first and foremost we are divine beings, we lose sight of our inner judgement as well. Then no longer do we know what is real and what is not. When we become dependent on externals – whether they be material possessions or teachers – we are asleep to our life's potential. Sometimes we can remain in this state for months, sometimes for years or decades even. How tragic it is when we end up living out our whole lives in this manner.

We must never forget that our mission is to develop an intimate understanding of the Divine. Everything else is secondary. We must also bear in mind that those who had little in-sight or common sense in this life don't suddenly become all-wise and all-knowing when they pass over. There are many mischievous beings who delight in preying upon those who lack discrimination, pretending to be those they are not. And so whatever messages we receive, always they must be weighed against our common sense, and against the truth of our own inner voice. If something doesn't strike the right chord, then no matter how spectacular or convincing the information, we must discard it.

Choosing our teachers wisely

There are many who claim to have the truth, yet we must always examine what is placed before us with great care. In recent years there has been a disturbing tendency to appropriate sacred laws and manipulate the universe for material gain. Those who promote these teachings are often extremely charismatic. They might even be psychically adept and well able to impress large crowds, yet rarely do they focus on things that are truly sacred.

When, by contrast, we examine the lives of the great teachers, their work is profound. Always they point their disciples to the Divine, rather than tailoring their message to reflect the mood of the times. When one has the privilege to sit in their presence, it is an exquisite experience. Their ego is transparent to the point of being almost, if not entirely, non-existent. One cannot help but sense the Divine around them, because theirs is a oneness with the Great Spirit that lies far beyond everyday words and deeds — it just *is*.

So if our lives are touched by the otherworldly, let us scrutinise what we have been given. Let us decide for our selves if it provides true in-sight, and let us also examine our state of mind before we come to any conclusions. Are we feeling out of sorts and in need of excitement, or are we in a frame of mind that will enable us to recognise authentic guidance when it comes our way?

Of course there are times when we need clarification, but we must not rely on externals to see us through. There is no soul development if we don't learn to think and act for our selves. Spiritual understanding is like any other, it takes time and experience to develop. The more we use it, the more adept we become.

When we seek sacred guidance, we are accessing the very power and wisdom of the universe. When we have the courage to trust this guidance, we become strong, and with this strength comes the ability to love and to be wise.

On Guidance

A prayer to help us gain the guidance we need

'O, Great Spirit, help me to access the guidance I need, so that always I can progress my life's quest to become wise. Help me to discern the guidance that is real from that which might seem genuine. Help me also to hold my life a little more lightly, knowing that whatever guidance I need will come to me as long as I keep an open mind. And in holding myself lightly, may I then become more spontaneous, so that I might enjoy more fully this adventure called life.'

Where Do We Live?

*Whatsoever things are true, whatsoever things are honest,
whatsoever things are just, whatsoever things are pure,
whatsoever things are lovely . . . think on these things.*
St Paul

Understanding our soul vibration

How might we describe the space we occupy? We are not talking about where we live so much as the energy in which we choose to live our daily lives. Basically the level we have reached as souls at this point in time is our souls' attainment or vibration. Our soul vibration is the very real space we occupy. It is the energetic frequency we are living in at this present moment, and it is the energy that we carry with us throughout life and into death, and beyond it. This doesn't mean our vibration is fixed. Each and every day our thoughts and actions and our intent affect our vibration. If the sum total of our thoughts and actions is positive, then they will positively affect our soul vibration, and vice versa. And so we take the benefits or otherwise of our soul's attainment with us wherever we go.

The more we advance on our life's quest, the lighter and higher our soul vibration. And the higher our vibration, the easier it is for us to navigate our way through life, because our energies are more closely aligned to our sacred essence. It informs our ability not only to cope with life, but to enjoy it and to make progress.

This is why we might have an advanced soul living in simple circumstances in an energy of perpetual bliss, while another soul who has every luxury and accolade may be living in an energy without joy or fulfilment. We don't have to look very hard for the latter examples. Life is full of the haunted, hunted kind – they dominate our corporate cultures and our political process, they fill our movie screens and popular music culture. And if we do not take care we can find our selves aspiring to the same soul-deadening values that prevent these individuals from realising their soul potential.

The effect of the energies within and around us

If we hope to make the most of our time here on Earth, we need to pay close attention to the energy in which we live, because the cumulative effect of this energy affects the soul vibration we attain during this lifetime. Once we know this we realise the importance of nurturing and protecting our soul's vibration against harmful or unhelpful influences, which include anything from watching a violent movie to being around someone who is very negative. Only when the conditions are conducive to raising our energy can we continue to grow in wisdom and in Light.

Hundreds of times each day we make choices that affect the way we think and behave. These choices have a direct bearing on our energy, which in turn impacts on our soul vibration. Buddhist teachings talk of the many seeds we plant – seeds that originate from our thoughts and from what we say and do. And as time passes these seeds grow, until eventually we reap the harvest of our deeds and intentions. For some the harvest brings great joy, while for others it is a blighted harvest that has grown out of negativity and fear.

If we are constantly angry or depressed, then our soul vibrations are naturally lower and denser, and this is the energy we will continue to attract to us. Then as our inner Light grows dim we become paralysed by our fear and uncertainty and find it hard to make progress. Often it will feel as if we are wading through deep water, or as if we are having the life crushed out of us. When we are feeling this way, it is a sure indicator that all is not well and that we need to lighten up, in every sense of the word. Once we are aware of the impact of our thoughts and actions, however, we can start to be more aware of what we invite into our lives.

Not all the difficult things we experience are a result of our negativity. There will be times that stretch the best of us. Then we realise that it is not what happens to us so much as how we deal with it that affects our soul's progress. We each have our own way of handling the circumstances in our lives – some of us cope and thrive while others seem to almost drown at every turn. When we come across accounts of the lives of the saints, we learn that regardless of their many hardships they regarded their life's journey as deeply blessed. Their soul vibrations were far higher and lighter than most, so in spite of the immense difficulties they often faced, the dark aspects of life weren't able to touch them. Their beings were illumined and so illumination was their experience.

THE IMPACT OUR SOUL VIBRATION HAS ON OUR LIFE

Have you ever noticed how a certain friend or family member has a life filled with unnecessary drama to the point that they seem almost to be a magnet for disaster? This is because the energy of doom and gloom has become the norm for this person. This is something more pervasive than having a run of bad luck, it is a lifetime's pattern of high and unrelenting drama that has become a habit.

When we live unconsciously it is hard for us to create a more positive energy around us. We become so used to the pain and the discomfort we begin to define our selves by it – this becomes the filter through which we experience life, and this in turn informs our thoughts and actions. Unless we form a strong connection with the Divine Light within and lift our vibrations, the odds are we will continue to experience a great deal of drama.

We are responsible for the energy in which we choose to live. We can lead lives that are scattered and distracted, or we can gather our energy about us and strengthen our being with all that is Light, so that increasingly we are protected from those things that get us down and hold us back.

Progressing beyond the unhelpful energies in our life

When we are aware of the importance of our soul vibration and of the differing energies that surround us, we can begin to move beyond those things that limit us. We then see our reactions to situations in a new light. We might have had a rough patch at work or in a relationship that has dented our self-confidence, and without even realising it we have started to become resentful of the achievements of others or overly critical of those we love. Or we might have become so weary that we have stopped making an effort, and before we know it everything around us seems lacklustre. But when we see these negative energy patterns in our lives, we are able to begin to move beyond them.

We do this by becoming attuned to the very real effects the differing energies have on our being. Take a moment to recall a happy occasion, and as you bring it to mind, allow it to come alive. Feel it energising every cell of your body. Experience what it is like to live within a lighter energy than you are normally accustomed to. This is the kind of energy you can enjoy permanently, if you so choose. And if you were to continue to inhabit an energy as light as this, over time your soul vibration would be raised also.

If by contrast you think about all the deadlines and as yet incomplete tasks you need to undertake, about all the things you still want out of life and haven't got, how different the energy! As you immerse your selves in these thoughts, every part of your being contracts. Your vision fades and you are left feeling anxious once more. No longer does the world seem such a safe place, nor do you feel you have a clear place within it. When you are in this space you become clouded, making it hard for your soul to take flight.

Being more aware of the company we keep

Once we realise the impact external energies have on us at every level of our being, we can take a serious look at how these various energies are played out in our lives. We can see how almost sponge-like we are when we take on the issues of those around us, how we absorb their fears, or how time and again we react negatively to those we distrust or dislike.

It is all too easy to pick up on the concerns and petty gripes of others. When we do so, we diminish the Divine Light of our inner being, then we end up sharing the anxieties and preoccupations of others and their lower vibrations as well. Always we must remember that even when we are surrounded by those who are angry or depressed, it is still our *choice* to take on their lower energies or to be unaffected by them.

How best to nurture our whole being

Too often we absorb the negativity around us, not because we are stupid or hopeless but because we don't realise how highly receptive we are physically, mentally and spiritually. We assume that as long as we feed and water our bodies, as long as we manage to give our selves a decent amount of sleep and exercise, we are looking after our selves, when in actual fact we haven't even begun to nurture our selves.

When we learn to live within our own space, to treat it as sacred and to guard it and care for it, no longer will we be so affected by the lower energies that bombard us daily. We can then make the changes in our lives that are needed by embracing our sacred practice, so that daily our connection with the Light increases. We do this by being more aware of our thoughts and actions, conscious or otherwise, by becoming attuned to the energies and emotions around and within us, by embracing those things that sustain us, and by having the in-sight to discard all those things that do not.

Right speech and right action and right thoughts (meaning 'good' speech, actions and thoughts) are all cornerstones of Buddhist teachings, not just because these are appropriate things to do but because they positively impact on our soul vibration and on our progress towards lightness of being. We have all said and done things that are unworthy, but we don't have to continue down this path. The more we persist with our intention to get our every thought and word and deed right, the more we will succeed.

It is important to take an active role in nurturing our souls so we can start to make a conscious choice to be enfolded by the Light and to remain within this energy come what may. When we begin to honour our own space as sacred, our minds, bodies and spirits are uplifted, as are our soul vibrations. Again this is about realising who we really are.

Our journey towards awakening is an awesome one, and Archbishop Desmond Tutu explains this beautifully when he tells of a chicken who day after day wandered about the farmyard pecking around in the dirt. Then one day a stranger arrived at the farm, and seeing the chicken he picked it up and threw it into the sky, pointing it in the direction of the sun. As the chicken was flung high into the air, he opened his wings without effort. He had never flown any distance before, but now he felt as if he were able to fly forever. Higher and higher he soared, and as he did so every cell in his being soared with him. When he looked back he couldn't believe his eyes, because his were not the wings of a chicken but the wings of an eagle. Only then did he realise who he really was. All the years he had spent pecking around in the dirt, he had never given any thought to who he was. He had never seen the vast expanse of the heavens, nor the welcome light of the sun, but in this moment it was as if this was all he had ever known. Higher and higher he flew until he became one with the Light.

This exquisite tale lays out the map of the human quest. It can take us years before we recognise our true selves and where we are heading. Yet once we understand this, everything changes, then our only desire is to head for the Light and embrace that which we already are.

As we begin to respond to the power and love of the universe, we learn to harness the many feelings and emotions we possess. And instead of being a slave to our anger or our fear or despair, we learn to master these energies so that we can experience all that is beautiful and true in life. Then, like the chicken, we can cease pecking around in the minutiae and discover our eagle natures.

When the pupil is ready, the master will come

When we are ready to move beyond our limitations, all we need do is ask the Great Spirit for assistance and direction will follow. Then even our most simple needs will be met. Notice it is our *needs* we are talking about, not the long list of things we would like. Suddenly we will stumble across the lecture we need to hear, or someone will tell us of a book that has helped them and which in turn helps us.

The more we open our selves up to these seeming coincidences, the more they will occur. These are very real markers that the universe places before us to help us navigate our way through the perplexities of life. These many synchronicities often come from left of field, and if we take note of them, they will lead us to a place where we can become wise.

Life's Synchronicities are sent to inspire and to heal

Some years ago I remembered a friend, Kayt, whom I had let down. She had been going through a crisis and had looked to me for support, but as I had just had an operation I was too fragile to respond. Instead of explaining myself I had avoided the issue and so our friendship had faded. A number of years had passed and I was living on the other side of the world when I decided to write to Kayt and apologise. Beginning the letter was hard, but once it was finished the relief was overwhelming. I sealed the letter and placed it in my bag, intending to post it on the way to work. When I arrived at the mailbox the letter was gone. It had obviously fallen out of my bag.

I was close to despair, but then I realised that if I believed in the universe I needed to trust that the letter would be posted. I wanted to believe that miracles can happen, yet I had lost my letter in a city of millions during rush hour. I gave myself a week to see what would happen – just enough time for a letter to wing its way across the world and to get a response.

The days dragged by and there was no letter. Then on the seventh day there was a letter from Kayt – my letter had arrived the day before her mother died. I was shocked and exhilarated that of all the years I had had the opportunity to apologise my letter came when Kayt needed it most, enabling me to finally be there for her in some small way.

As the Light grows within us, so we are able to illuminate the way for others. Then, even when people around us get sick or when those we love pass away, still we can enhance the Light in the world with a kind word or supportive deed, or by displaying unwavering goodness in the face of adversity. We can only do this, however, when we have the guiding Light to see us home.

A prayer to help us take care of our soul vibration

'O, Great Spirit, it is easy to become tired and distracted, and to allow those energies into my life that are not good for me. Help me to create a sacred space within and around me, so that I might support and enhance my soul vibration as I continue to progress towards lightness of being.'

WHAT IS THE DARKNESS?

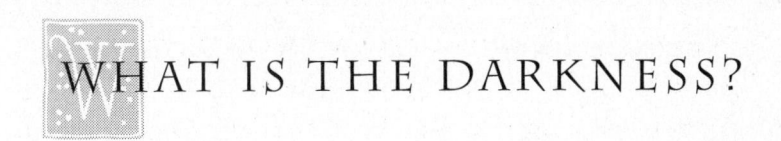

The dark is what makes the Light utterly precious.

RECOGNISING THE DARKNESS AROUND US

Although we have made reference to the darkness it is helpful to explore what we mean by this, because we need to recognise the many faces of the dark and comprehend its purpose in our lives. This is not always a comfortable topic, because there is a great deal of fear attached to the dark. Yet unless we move beyond our apprehensions, we are unlikely to reach a space in life that will empower and liberate us. It is important we realise that the darkness is the absence of Light. And so all the fearful notions we might hold of the darkness are a reflection of what it might feel like to live in a space without Light.

My own childhood was characterised by endless sermons on hell and damnation. The church elders, it seemed, were obsessed with evil. Life was presented as a never-ending struggle between darkness and light, and caught somewhere in the middle of this huge cosmic battle were you and I, the hapless members of humankind. Yet from a very young age I could not accept that human life was the vale of tears that had been depicted, and everything I have subsequently learned supports this. When we become preoccupied with the darkness, we allow it more prominence than it rightly deserves. We cannot grow as spiritual beings when we allow our selves to be distracted or intimidated by evil. Our quest is to enhance the Light in our selves, until we too are filled with Light.

This does not mean we should be complacent or foolhardy in life. Always we must be vigilant, because the dark is mesmeric, addictive even. Often it meets us where we least expect it. We catch it in snippets of gossip that expose and exploit the fragilities of those around us. We invite it in when we treat some people more kindly than others, or when we are selfish or self-seeking. Even our magazines and films and newspapers are frequently laced with darkness, with their sensationalist accounts of abuse and deep despair. And if we are not careful we too can end up becoming addicted to the thrill of the latest scandal or disaster, until we are no longer aware of other ways of living and being.

No one who has travelled far on life's path would dream of inviting the darkness of anger and dysfunction in, because it contributes nothing towards our lightness of being. When we get caught up in self-defeating energies there is little in our lives to sustain us, and so sooner or later we become bored and restless and resentful. Then when life gets too much for us we distract our selves with sex and work and shopping, with drugs and alcohol to combat our emptiness. We become dependent on the very things that open us up psychically, which make us even more vulnerable to all the negative forces around us.

Transcending our woundedness

Today many of us spend a great deal of time focusing in on our woundedness in therapy and in endless conversations with friends. We concentrate on those parts of our lives that aren't working, instead of reminding our selves of all those things in our lives that are joyous and that do work. Of course therapy has value, as does the support of our friends, but there comes a time when we need to transmute those things that hurt and disappoint us into something positive and worthwhile.

Human life is not an impossibly cruel quest. We haven't been dumped here on Earth, then left alone to survive the many evils we encounter. We arrive on this planet clothed in flesh and in our own divinity. We carry within us the sacred Light of wisdom and truth and love. Our brief mission is to discover the Light within us and how we might best use our knowledge of the Light to reach our full magnificence.

Coming to terms with our wrongdoing

Of course there will be times when we meet things that are dark, and while we cannot ignore them, we must not allow them to distract us either, because the dark is insidious. We are drawn in through our own fears and anxieties and resentments. If we allow our own negativity to go unchecked, who is to say where it might lead us? Hitler wasn't born Führer of Germany, nor Stalin the iron fist of Russia. These men were opportunists, who gathered the weak around them until they became terrible forces to be reckoned with. We have the capacity to hurt our selves and others, or to produce something of lasting worth. The choice is ours.

We strengthen our selves against the negative tendencies inside and around us when we have the courage to own the darkness within our unworthy thoughts and deeds, and to work on these things. The less vulnerable we are, the more progress we make. Desperate situations such as those brought about by Hitler and Stalin were a result of people's inability to keep the negative energies of life in check.

Seeing into the heart of darkness

We must take good care of the negative impulses we all experience, because the energies of fear and anger and disappointment belong to the darkness. They belong to those who are as yet unawakened to the divinity that lies within. Once we grasp this, we realise that whatever the issues we struggle with in our daily lives, they are no different from those that create wars and suffering of every kind. If we destroy what is good and beautiful around us, we create fear and hate as well.

It is important for us to realise that when people are operating from a very low vibration, they are doing so because that is the soul space they inhabit. Whatever pain or fear they give out is a reflection of the much greater pain or fear that resides within them. Being aware of this means that whenever we meet dissension in relationships or in families or at work, we are more able to see what is actually going on. We can then begin to view these dark energies with the detachment they deserve. One of the many ways we get drawn into situations that are not good for us is when we get emotionally involved. And so the more detachment we have, the more effective we will be in dealing with such situations. The darkness can and will hinder our journey, but only if we allow our selves to be nudged off course. We are not battling a force we have no tools for, we are testing our ability to hold the Light of goodness come what may.

Dealing with the darkness

When the forces of the dark are gathering we do need to be ready, because these lower energies are very draining. We must never respond from our ego, because flight and fight is all the ego understands. And when we allow our ego to take charge, we end up embracing the very energies we seek to combat. When times are tough we need to work even harder to uphold the Light. Again this brings us back to the importance of our sacred practice, because it is through our practice that we can access all the courage and in-sight we need to see us through. The challenges that the darkness presents us with are like the sand in the oyster – they can be hugely frustrating, but they can also create the pearl of great value.

When we are in the thick of things it is easy to be overwhelmed by dramatic turns of event. It is useful to remind our selves that whatever the drama we are facing, we are working from very old scripts. No matter how terrible the circumstance, it has already been played out many times down through the ages. We can respond in the same ill-informed way many have done before us, or we can seize the chance to rewrite the script, change the outcome and reach a place of greater illumination.

If we are to combat the dark we do need to find new ways of dealing with old problems. Always we must use our inner wisdom so that we can arrive at an outcome which is good and true. We can only do this, however, when we are informed by the Light. When we face life's dark moments with courage and in-sight, strange and wonderful things will happen. Not only are we able to be more even-handed towards those who infuriate or intimidate us, we are able to reach wonderfully creative solutions as well.

We must deal with the darkness judiciously, so that we have the chance to reach a place of extraordinary compassion and wisdom. We are then able to pray for those who hurt us, asking that they too might be released from their suffering. This is what the Master Jesus did when he asked that those who had tortured and crucified him be forgiven. This is a profound gesture, and while it lies far beyond our everyday concept of forgiveness, it can and will transform lives.

The redeeming power of the Light
There are times when we all feel overwhelmed by the desperate acts that are taking place on the planet. It is important that we do not dwell on these things, lest we end up drowning in our anger and despair. Instead we need to continue to hold a space of goodness and Light. When we are able to do so, we do our selves and all living things great service, because always the Light will outshine the darkness.

This also means that even for those who commit unspeakable acts of inhumanity there is always a way back to wholeness. This might not impress those who seek vengeance, until we are reminded how comforting it is to know that in spite of all our flaws and uncertainties, we too can have access to universal love and healing.

There will be times when we forget the awesome power of our divine selves, when we behave badly or thoughtlessly. When this happens there is no point in wallowing in recrimination or self-pity. We are here to learn and grow, and if we are smart we will learn from our mistakes and seek to rectify them, then move on. End of story.

Getting the help we need
The darkness can and will paralyse us – it will distort our judgement, but only if we allow it to do so. When we are under pressure it is important that we don't try to go it alone. Instead we need to intensify our sacred practice and meditate at least once a day. The more we persist with our sacred practices, the easier it will be for us to get back on track and stay there.

What Is the Darkness?

During these times of pressure we need also to seek additional silence and space, so we can benefit from the promptings of our inner voice, and from the positive, Light-filled sources around us. It is often wise to seek out a good healer at such times. It also helps to visualise our selves surrounded by Light at the beginning of and throughout the day.

Recognising the many faces of the darkness

We meet darkness in many guises. While those things that are patently wrong are easy to pick, the darkness of ignorance and wrongdoing is not always so straightforward. Sometimes the dark places possibilities before us that seem so palatable that we don't even pause to think before reaching out for them. This kind of darkness is often related to expediency. It surfaces within relationships and families, and within organisations big and small, and it seeks our willingness to act without question, to take the line of least resistance. Then we find our selves supporting wrong decisions, simply to keep others happy or to avoid any hassles, forgetting that all unworthy deeds feed the darkness of ignorance and fear.

Then there is the face of darkness that is the most deadly of all. This is the face of the dark which meets us when we least expect it, catching us unawares. It is the face of the dark with which we feel most comfortable, because it speaks to us in a voice that articulates our deepest desires and whatever it presents us with will seem so right it will feel like a gift from the gods, when in fact what it offers is very wrong. When this aspect of the dark seeks us out, we need to exercise all the willpower and conscience we possess. This is the face of the dark that has brought many of the world's greatest leaders to their knees. More than likely we will find our selves willing to respond, to do whatever is required of us. To resist will probably be one of the most difficult decisions we have ever made, and yet as painful as this might be, it is nowhere near as painful as life would be, should we give in to temptation.

A good friend found herself in this very situation. Her husband was facing financial and career problems, and nothing she could do or say was right. So unbearable had things become that she had started to look for her own apartment. Then she met a male colleague who had everything she didn't have. He too was married and extremely unhappy, and not only did he share her interests and values, he was clearly attracted to her and made no secret of the fact. Everything he said and did pulled at her heartstrings. And while she struggled to keep the family finances afloat, she was painfully aware that if she were with this man she would never have to worry about money again.

Yet as promising as the possibility of this new relationship appeared, she felt as if she were standing on the edge of an abyss. Her inner guidance was to pass on this relationship, and after days of soul-searching she managed to do just that. It was the hardest decision she had ever made. For the first few days after her decision she felt even worse at letting go this opportunity. Then about a week later she woke up to find her anguish gone, and in its place was an immense sense of relief. What astounded her most was the way her husband began to change. As she became more committed to the relationship, he became more relaxed and appreciative, and he even insisted on getting a second job to pay off his debts. They now have a relationship that is strong and happy, while the other man turned out to be serially unfaithful and deeply insecure.

When we want things too much, we are at our most vulnerable. And should we succumb to temptation, then vampire-like the darkness will claim us for itself. It will feed off our energies and distort our judgement. We will then find our selves getting rid of people who stand in our way, or depriving others of their rightful place, or entering illicit relationships and partnerships. We might well produce valid reasons for doing what we do, but deep down we know differently. When we betray or defraud another, we also betray our selves and no joy will follow. The examples are endless, but the end result is the same. The darkness of wrongdoing brings no peace. It simply leaves us hungry and desperate for more.

THE GIFT OF THE DARKNESS
When we succumb to our ignorance we are often blind to the consequences that will surely follow. Yet if we are prepared to confront our mistakes, we will begin to attract experiences to us that will take us beyond our ignorance. And so out of our darkest actions, out of our loss of faith and vision, we learn we have more strength and more resilience than we thought possible.

There is not a great spirit on Earth that has not trodden the dark places in life at some stage in the evolution of their soul. What sets them apart from the rest is that having come through life's dark moments they give thanks for all they have learned, and then seek to share these things with others.

When asked if her holocaust experiences had left her without hope, an elderly Jewish lady said that it had made life infinitely more precious. Of course she would have preferred not to have had such a hellish experience, but having done so she was able to recognise that her life had far greater piquancy than would otherwise have been the case.

Darkness and Light don't merely co-exist. They are part of a greater, richer whole. And so instead of fearing the dark, we should see it for what it is, and learn all we can from it. Often it is not until we have experienced a bad partnership or ill health that we can appreciate a loving relationship or the blessings of good health. When we can view the dark times in our lives this way, then we too can be greatly blessed by them.

THE HEALING POWER OF THE DARKNESS

The darkness is not always hostile, it can be a great friend, especially when we need to withdraw and allow the next stage of our physical, mental or spiritual metamorphosis to take place. Often, mistakenly, we view the quiet periods of our lives as dull or depressing, or as a complete waste of time. Yet just as the seed lies dormant in the depths of the earth, we also need time for consolidation and rest before we can successfully re-emerge and embrace the next chapter of our lives.

So just as we rested in the darkness of our mother's womb, we need to have time out now and again, so that we can then emerge renewed by the process. This kind of darkness is something else, it is the womb-time of existence that is both gentle and profound. It is out of this darkness that we are shaped and sustained.

A prayer for when life is overwhelming

'O, Great Spirit, things are hectic right now and I can't see my way clear. Help me to move beyond all the busyness and confusion, so that I can draw strength and guidance from Your Divine Presence. As I stand here in this moment I ask that Your Divine Love may now enclose me, that Your Divine Light may now illuminate me, and that Your Divine Peace may now infuse every part of me.

What Is the Darkness?

'As I consciously invite these energies in, I ask that they be anchored deep within my being, so that they may transform me utterly. In experiencing all that these qualities bring, I am reminded that I AM Love, I AM Light, I AM Peace. Help me to live in Your Love, in Your Light, in Your Peace today and always.'

1 Inhabiting Sacred Space

Honouring the space we occupy
We need the Sacred. We need it as much as we need food and shelter. We need it because it nurtures us physically, mentally, spiritually, because it is who we are in essence, and because it is our bridge to the Divine. Recognising this, how can we move beyond the distractions of the material world to create a sacred space around and inside of us? How can we cocoon our selves within an energy that will sustain us through good times and bad?

In times past a great deal of effort was spent tending places that were deemed sacred, and when we visit these sacred locations even today we can still experience the exceptional energies to be found there. Our mission is to expand this possibility and enhance the Sacred wherever we might be, because *all* space has the potential to be sacred and to embody the Light.

Sadly many of us have come to regard our personal space as mundane, and so that tends to be our life experience. Yet those who are successful on life's quest know what they need to flourish, and they use this knowledge to enhance the space they occupy, by inviting the lighter, higher energies to be present there. And because the space they inhabit supports them, they are then able to live lives that are exceptional.

Part of the challenge of being here is in learning to adjust to the heavier energies of this plane of existence. This is why, in part, the birth process can be deeply traumatic, and why the energies that surround us can seem hard at times. The lighter the energies around us the better, because this is what we as souls are used to. When we find our selves yearning for a freedom that we can't articulate, we are in fact seeking the freedom of spirit we remember at a soul level – we are yearning for the Light.

When we do begin to wake up to the energies around us, we realise that we need to pay particular care to our selves and our environment. Often we forget that both are equally important. We can put a lot of effort into raising the energy in our homes and workplaces, but this will have little impact on our lives if we don't continue to enhance the Light within us. And when we fail to keep our thoughts and emotions in check, we contaminate the atmosphere in which we are living, and that doesn't help us much either.

In seeking to live within a sacred space, we need to realise that we play a key role in maintaining or destroying the very energies we seek to immerse our selves in. We need to step back and observe our lives dispassionately, so we can begin to see the people and situations that uplift us and those that don't. And in seeing this, we must then make a conscious effort to lift our energy and awareness above the concerns of the moment, so that negative energies do not get the chance to take root in our lives and our being.

READING THE SPACE AROUND US
How then do we support and enhance our soul vibration? We can begin by becoming aware of the textures of space around us.

Sometimes we can find our selves somewhere that appears pleasant, but which feels vaguely depressing or hostile even. As we explore this space, we realise just how deceptive appearances can be.

Everything we do and think and say is energy, and over time the accumulation of these energies becomes imprinted on the space around us. While some energies are uplifting many are not, and without even realising it we might be living in the kind of energies we can well do without.

A few years ago my company moved to a dream location, yet from the moment I arrived in my new workspace I began to feel anxious and depressed. I had no idea what was wrong, apart from the fact that I was tired and had a lot of work on. Then I realised I had inherited the office that had been used to hire and fire people, and clearly the residue of all that hurt remained. At the first possible moment I cleaned every surface, burnt sage and then invited the Great Spirit to bless the place. The energy in my office was immediately transformed. It took several days, however, before I felt totally energised, because my body was still processing the effects of the negative energy I had absorbed.

Overhauling our personal space

One of the best ways to refine our physical space is to learn how to spring-clean it. To do this we need to set aside some time when we can work without interruption. A couple of hours on the weekend is perfect. The more relaxed we are the better. Then as we begin to look around we will start to see where the energy is heavy or cluttered or neglected, and where it is light and happy. It is important to look at each room as a whole, as well as different parts of the room, because the energy can differ markedly from one part of a room to another.

Once we are finished, we then have a map of action. We know the bookshelves and cupboards that need sorting and cleaning, and the areas that need more sunshine and fresh air. Where the space is dark or depressing we might consider moving the furniture around, or finding clever ways to attract more light into gloomy corners with carefully placed mirrors. Adding colour can help and is easily done with the addition of cushions or scatter rugs, or by whatever inspires us. We might also give some thought to enhancing this space with sacred music or by burning essential oils.

Sacred objects to enhance our space

Sacred objects can also have a profound effect on the energy around us. These things can never be a substitute for the Divine, but they can help bring about profound shifts in the energies of our homes and workplaces. A sacred object can be anything from a poster or painting, a poem or a statuette that makes our soul sing.

It might feel right to position this object in a prominent place in our home, or to display it more privately. When we position our sacred object, it helps to do so with the clear intention that it will fill this space with Love and Light. Mindful of the greater good, we can also ask that anyone who looks upon this object will also be blessed.

This is not about filling our homes and workplaces with objects, nor about gathering sacred objects for superstitious ends. In the past people collected all sorts of paraphernalia in the hope that nothing bad would befall them, not realising that the objects themselves were of no value, apart from being pointers to the Divine.

Even the most humble space can be transformed by the sparing use of sacred objects. At one stage a corner of our garden was very gloomy, so we bought a tiny stone statue of the Lord Buddha, blessed it and placed it in that part of the garden. Within days the energy around that whole area had lifted, and in the weeks and months that followed the plants around the statue began to flourish. To our great joy we discovered that the flowers lasted longer here than anywhere else in the garden. We were also delighted to find that children were naturally drawn to the statue.

More recently I found a beautiful stone angel that seemed to radiate peace and love. It now stands in one corner of our tiny garden. We can see it from our front gate, and whenever we return home it greets us with a gentle smile, reminding us of divine love and tranquillity. On one level the angel is simply a carved lump of stone, yet on another it helps transport all who see it beyond the pettiness and freneticism of everyday life to a space that is far more profound.

Sacred objects have the ability to lift our hearts and souls, but we should never become dependent on them, nor should we worship them. These can become tools to strengthen our sense of purpose and our vision, but they cannot undertake the quest for us.

Learning how to smudge

Every year we should also cleanse our home and workspace by smudging and drumming and praying to the Great Spirit. We do this to consciously cleanse the energies of these places and to fill them with Light. When we do so we enter the realm of all that is deeply sacred, because we are inviting the Divine into our life and living space. To do so we must honour this opportunity and accord it the profound respect it is due. This means that we only seek to enter this space when we are able to set aside the concerns of the outer world, and when we are present enough to be able to invite the Sacred in. It is helpful to have showered beforehand and to wear fresh clothes. Ideally the space we seek to work on will have already been cleaned.

To smudge we use a bundle of dried sage bound with twine. A number of cultures use sage at the commencement of their ceremonies to define a sacred space. Practised with care and genuine intent, smudging will cleanse the energy of a particular physical space. To begin we take up our smudge stick and stand for a moment in complete silence, as we allow our attention to come into the room. Then, as we follow our breath slowly in and out, we allow all thoughts to settle. When we are ready we might like to offer up the following prayer:

> '*O, Great Spirit, I honour Your presence here and ask that with Your help this space be filled with the energies of Love and Light, so that all who dwell here may be greatly blessed. And as these divine energies fill this space, I ask that they might also enter my being and illuminate every part of me, so that I too may embrace my life's journey towards enlightenment more fully.*'

Light the sage stick at one end. After the initial burst of flames, allow it to settle down and smoulder. Once the sage is smouldering we can start to move through the space concerned, holding the sage stick before us. As we allow its fragrance to fill the air, we hold the words Love and Light in our hearts, or if we prefer we can say them out loud as we move around. It is important not to rush this process. When one area feels complete, we can then move on to the next. When we are finished we can then return to the place where we began and stand for a moment in silence, so that we can become more aware of the new energies that now infuse this space. When we are ready, we might like to close with the following prayer:

> 'O, Great Spirit, I thank you from the bottom of my heart for Your presence here today. I thank You for the sacred Love and Light You have brought here. I pray that I may honour this space in all that I may think and say and do. I now undertake to nurture and enhance the Love and Light here and within my own being. Thank You for the gift of my life, for all that this space has brought to my life.'

When we smudge we create an extraordinary space for ourselves, and while there is no need to smudge every week, it is a good idea to smudge when we get the urge to do so. If there seems no particular reason to smudge for a while, then why not smudge at significant times in the year, such as New Year or the change of seasons? Once the space has been smudged, it is important to maintain the sacredness of this place, and give thanks for all that is received as a result of this.

USING DRUMMING TO CLEAR SPACE

Drumming can also be a powerful medium in energy cleansing. If there is a drum to hand, then after blessing the instrument and seeking the assistance of the Great Spirit to fill the space with Light and Love, sound the drum throughout each room. The areas that feel flat will need more concerted drumming until the energy shifts. As we drum we simply focus on creating a space of Light and Love. When we are finished we will notice a definite shift in the energy, particularly in the areas where the energy had become stagnant.

If we don't have access to a drum or sage stick, we can still follow the format of the smudging ceremony with the opening and closing prayers, and by moving through the space mindfully, as we invite the energies of Love and Light to be present there. The important thing is that we consciously invite these energies into the space concerned, with the clear intention of allowing them to take up residence.

Nurturing our sacred space

Once we have cleansed and blessed our space we need to be judicious in our use and maintenance of it, so that we retain the higher energy we have invited in. This means taking care of the energies we allow to enter into these *living* spaces. It is always good to have joyous events in our homes, and to fill them with people of like mind. The more we do this, the more we add to the Light of our living space. We can also enhance the atmosphere in our homes with beautiful music and with silence and spaciousness.

We can still invite those who need the solace or the benefit of a lighter, higher energy into our space. When we do so it helps to envisage them surrounded and suffused with Light, and to visualise the same for our selves and our space. Should the energy feel heavier when they are gone, all we need do is open a door or a window and invite in the fresh air and the sunshine. Should the tension persist, then it helps to burn sweet grass, a dried grass used by Native Americans, which is an excellent tool when used with prayer. To re-dedicate our living space to the Light. If sweet grass isn't available, then why not use essential oils?

Always we must remind our selves that we need to inhabit a space that nurtures our inner voice and vision. This positive energy will then flow through to the rest of our lives, giving us more peace and purpose, more joy and a great deal more in-sight than we had before. When the atmosphere around us is as it should be, our sacred practice will become easier as well.

Dealing with those who drain us

For those who are negative and depressing in our lives, apart from asking how much time we want to spend around these people, we need to think carefully about where we meet. It is far better to get together in an uplifting location. This way we are more able to remain within our own higher energy and to assist in their healing as well. Again before we meet we need to surround our selves with Light and to consciously surround them with all the Light and Love we are able, so that everyone will benefit from the time spent together.

Then as we meet we must ask only that the person be released to their highest good. It is not up to us to try and manipulate outcomes. Again this is about learning to let go and live lightly. There will be times when there is a dramatic improvement in those we are with, and times when we don't seem to be helping them at all. We might well need to encourage them to seek professional help. Whatever the outcome, we must continue to hold a good space for them. This means that whenever we think or speak of that person, we do so in a way that is loving and that assumes that sooner or later they too will experience the Light more fully in their own lives.

Spiritual growth and in-sight is an exhilarating experience. And when we allow our selves to live in a sacred space, profound things can and will begin to take place for us and for those around us.

Contemplations on our personal space

Find somewhere you enjoy, where you are able to be alone. Then, as you settle, allow your thoughts to slow as you bring your attention back into your body. Then, as you follow your breath slowly in and out, allow your thoughts to cease as you submerge yourself in this meditative space. Then, when you feel sufficiently settled, why not contemplate one or more of the following questions and see what inner guidance you receive?

- Which areas at home need me to work on them energetically?
- What changes might I make that will enhance these energies?
- What do I need to change about the way I care for this space that will ensure higher energies will be present there?
- Who are those who constantly drain me, and how best might I deal with them?
- Who are the people who inspire me?
- What kind of uplifting opportunities can I create with those I love in my home?

A prayer to help us attract the energy we need around us

'O, Great Spirit, help me to discover all the resources I need to enhance the space in which I live, so that my home becomes a sacred space.'

Entering the Silence

Waking up to the sounds around us
Noise has become such a constant in our lives that we tend not to notice it any more. Whether it is the roar of traffic or simply the hum of an electronic device it makes little difference – noise is noise. So accustomed have many of us become to noise that in those rare moments when we are alone, instead of relishing the opportunity for some quiet we turn on the sound system, or we pick up the phone. We retreat to those sounds that are familiar, not realising that many of the sounds that have become our comfort zone are our prison also.

We know that prolonged exposure to certain sounds can make us deaf, but there is a great deal more to the effects of sound on us than this. Sound is energy, and when we make a habit of turning on the walkman or TV, we are not only exposing our selves to thousands upon thousands of differing sounds, but their differing energies also. When we immerse our selves in mindless chat, in inane stories and conversations, we end up living in a state of perpetual distraction, where there is no room to think, let alone be.

Even the choice of words we expose our selves to can be critical. Words can encourage us to achieve all sorts of wonderful things we never thought possible, but they can also spark the slaughter of millions. Words are all around us, washing over us from the time we get up to the time we fall asleep. Most have no meaning for us – they are simply there. Whether we are aware of the effects of all this sound or not, it still affects every part of us. When we listen to contemporary songs, for example, often we are listening to words written out of extreme anger and violence and despair. Yet because the music carries us along, rarely do we realise that these are the very energies that cause the Sacred inside us to contract.

When we do become aware of the effects that all the words and sounds have on us, we can start to look at our daily diet of ads and news bulletins and music, and distinguish what is genuinely helpful and informative from what is not. We then learn to recognise the intrusive energies to which we expose our selves daily – energies that seek to persuade us to think this or do that; energies that over time numb our perceptions, and diminish our vision and spontaneity.

Inviting silence into our lives

Often what we need most in our frantic lives is some peace and quiet. The practice of silence is not about shutting our selves away from life, but about enriching our life experience so that it has more beauty and piquancy. No matter how busy we might be, there are still many ways we can create a quality of silence in our lives that will enfold us in its peace and wisdom. Then, the more silence becomes part of our lives, the more we are able to carry this energy with us out into the busy city streets, into meetings at work and gatherings with friends, allowing it to refresh and refocus us, so that we can deal with the stress and the freneticism with ease.

Even where the noise is unavoidable, instead of resisting it, when we make time to bathe our selves in silence, we can then move into the heart of that worrisome sound, then through and beyond it. We will then find that the effect that noise has on our being will be minimal.

There are few places in our day that would not benefit from silence. We can even practise it while driving. Not only will our stress levels drop, in the exquisite moments between thoughts we will have the time and space to enjoy what is going on inside and around us. As we sit at traffic lights, we can then take a moment to pause and just be, or to appreciate the play of light on the car or on surrounding buildings, or to watch storm clouds gathering overhead. When we are able to drive in silence, instead of it being a stressful experience, it can be an extension of all that we receive during meditation.

As we work with silence we come to realise that it is yet another manifestation of the sacred face of life, because when our minds are free we are able to appreciate the immense beauty and intricacy of life. We are able to absorb the unexpected qualities of our friends and family and workmates. Our hearts dance to note the rich texture of their hair, the rise and fall of their voices, or the fluidity of their movements. When we have time to be silent, we give our selves time to become centred as well. Then when we do spend time with others we enter a space that is more authentic, because we are no longer too tired or distracted to *be* there. How often in our busy lives do we end up drifting off when we are with those we love, scarcely hearing what they are saying? We are drifting because we are desperate for some silence and space.

The healing power of silence

In these days where loneliness is physical as well as mental and spiritual, an absence of words can be profoundly healing for those needing comfort. There is great healing to be had when we can move beyond words and simply be *with* a person in need. We experienced this for our selves as children, when those who cared for us would gather us up in their arms when we were feeling tired or sad. These brief moments of nurture were infinitely precious, because we were enfolded in love.

The same is true of adults. We don't always want to keep going back over the same old ground, yet when we are faced with a highly emotional situation it can be tempting to fill the silence with words. When instead we can simply hold someone in our arms, or take their hand and just *be* with them in a shared moment of silence, we will meet that person in a far more genuine space than if we were to talk. We can also use our intimate relationship with silence to allow the other person to unburden themselves without interruption. We serve others best when we are able to sit in silence, listening intently, as we visualise the shared space enfolded in Light and Love. Then if we need to respond we can ask that whatever we say will come from a place of deep wisdom and love. In the profound intimacy of these kinds of moments, the Silence enables us to connect soul to soul.

Enjoying a new relationship with sound

When we make a friend of silence we are able to have a new relationship with the sounds around us as well. Without even having to think about it, we begin to seek out the sounds that uplift and heal. Then, when we hear the cry of a bird or the dry rustle of leaves, these moments have such piquancy it is often as if we are experiencing them for the very first time. As our relationship with sound continues to deepen, so too does our response to it. Then, when we catch the sudden sigh of the wind or the cry of a newborn child, our heart explodes with the extraordinary beauty of these moments.

Those peoples who have remained close to nature often have such an intimate relationship with sound that they can hear all the sounds around them individually and collectively at the same time. And so they can hear a frog at the edge of a nearby lake at the same time they can hear the slow pad of a wolf and the persistent hum of insects and so on, even if they are coming from different directions.

Imagine the richness of life, if we too were able to absorb the sounds of nature so clearly and profoundly. This gives us a sense of just how expansive our life experience can be, and inspires us to awaken from the blanket of sound we have become familiar with, so that we too can appreciate the nuances of sound.

Deepening our experience of silence

After I had been working with the Silence for some time, I returned to the deserts of Utah and Colorado. The depth of silence to be found there was like entering the very heart of God. This is not something one says lightly, but there the silence was like no other. It took me far beyond my everyday self, linking me with that which is far greater than the individual I.

In this silence was Love beyond all imagining. There too lay the great wisdom and power of the universe. There resided the great I AM of creation that defies explanation, that just is. There was the balm that we, who have become so fragmented, crave for. Within this silence lay the essence of who we all are, because everything we need to know becomes apparent to us. Within the Silence of that vast place I *felt* whole. I *knew* who I was and nothing appeared more important than simply *being* who I was. And as all my freneticism and misconceptions dropped away, I came to realise that the whisper of God is just a heartbeat away, if we can but surrender our constant need to prove, to control and to analyse.

When I returned to everyday life, more than ever I could see and feel the effects that sound has on us. My heart sank as I watched people in restaurants and cafes barraged by radio and TV, absorbing the energy of thousands upon thousands of messages, along with their food. I watched parents sit down to eat with their children, without even a word being exchanged between them. As I observed all this going on around me, it was as if I was watching an enchantment so deep that those who were affected by it were experiencing little beyond life's most basic functions. And then I remembered how easy it was to come home to an empty house and put on the radio or TV, to keep disquieting thoughts at bay. When we have no sense of what the Silence has to offer, we have no reason to make it our own.

Allowing the Silence to transform us

The Silence has many gifts, regardless of how busy or stressed we might be. The important thing is to try it and see what happens. Why not make a commitment to yourself here and now to find moments in the day to come back to the centre, to be alone with your thoughts, to dream the big dreams?

Meditation is one of the most profound ways of entering the Silence, because it can take us to a deep place with ease. Once we know where this sacred space is, we can revisit it many times during the day. The more we are able to access this space, the more we can start to live in this space and make it our own.

For each of us, the practice of silence will be different.

It might mean taking time out to garden or paint, or to take regular walks in the park or luxuriate in the bath once or twice a week. Whatever silence you choose to embrace, allow yourself to enjoy and absorb the lighter energies that are here for you. Let them nurture and heal and fill you, so that you can enrich your every moment.

A prayer to help us invite the silence into our days

'O, Great Spirit, as I become more aware of the effect of sound in my life, help me to carve out the space I need to experience the awesome beauty and depth that Silence brings to our lives. Help me to embrace Silence and make it my own, so that I too may experience the all-encompassing calm and wisdom that quiet moments in the day bring. And as I make Silence my friend, may I learn to take its many gifts with me wherever I might be, so that I might bless the lives of those around me as well.'

UNCLUTTERING OUR LIVES

SEEING CONSUMERISM FOR WHAT IT IS
Whether or not we realise it, every single thing we own draws from our life force, because everything we have requires our attention. Each item of clothing we possess needs washing, our beds need to be made, our furniture dusted, our utensils washed and stacked, our floors cleaned and so on. Even if we are not overly solicitous towards the things we own, still we spend considerable time maintaining them. We need only see how we carve up our spare time to get a true sense of how much our possessions demand of us.

If we wish to achieve lightness of being it is vital that we are mindful of where we expend our life energy. This means that we need to give thought to *every* single thing we own and we seek to own, because if we don't we can find our selves drawn into the trap of working simply to be able to afford to consume. And when we get caught in this cycle of acquiring without thought, our lives become a never-ending treadmill of wanting and getting and wanting some more.

It then becomes a habit to allow ourselves to be diverted by everything that catches our eye, regardless of whether we need it or not. Then when the dark times come, as inevitably they do, we have no other solution available to us than to distract our selves from the misery of the moment. Shopping centres the world over are full of people attempting to buy their way out of loneliness, boredom or despair. This is no revelation, but what solution does shopping provide to life's penetrating questions? How can it point us in the right direction and liberate us from our deep sense of inadequacy?

There are few of us who can question the euphoria to be experienced when we have a shopping binge. While it is a thrill to gather up all the packages, often the new-found joy that comes with these purchases scarcely lasts the trip home. Once the buzz has faded, the shadows of doubt and despair return, causing us to feel even more empty than before.

Recognising the emptiness within

Of course we need to take physical care of our selves and those we love. The problem comes when these material goods become the only reason for living. Many of us live in a perpetual state of emptiness, and no matter which way we turn, nothing seems to fill the gaping hole deep inside us – not even the love of friends and family, financial security, or success in our chosen career. Yet often it is not until we are at a point of near despair that we are able to recognise how starved our lives are of joy and spontaneity, how lacking they are in terms of fulfilment. The more we accumulate, the more our lives become crowded if not downright suffocating. This is an uncomfortable space to inhabit. Once we realise just how empty our lives have become, our awareness can catapult us into the space where there is lasting joy and satisfaction.

We can only enjoy space in the fullest sense when we rid our selves of all those things we don't need. This doesn't mean that life has to be pinched and frugal, or that we have to give away everything we own, but most of us can benefit from travelling a great deal lighter. There is a very good reason why for centuries the best monastic traditions have emphasised the value of having few possessions, because it frees us up so we can enter another more meaningful layer of reality. And when we are able to pass on all those things we don't need, we not only give our selves the chance to breathe, we enrich the lives of others less fortunate than us.

Leaving the past behind

There is more to making space in our lives than simply creating room in our drawers and cupboards. We don't have to have lived long before the past can exert a subtle yet powerful hold on our lives so we need to examine the accumulation of our attitudes along with those of our possessions.

Some years ago I came across a suitcase packed with student clothes. There was no way I would wear any of these clothes again, but I couldn't bring myself to throw them out. What was it about my student days I couldn't let go of? Was it the spontaneity, the sheer aliveness of being young? Was it the passion, the idealism of those heady days that I clung to? Or was it the unwavering belief I once had in myself and my ability to make a difference?

The more I thought about this, the more I realised there were elements of all these reasons in my inability to throw the old clothes out. I had effectively packaged up a significant part of my life and locked it away. And although the opportunities for spontaneity and idealism hadn't disappeared from my life, my unwavering belief in myself had. That was the nub of it. Taking a deep breath, I ditched my clothes and began to work on my vision for the future.

There aren't many of us who aren't locked into some aspect of the past, who don't spend our time reliving an old relationship or job. We have all been guilty of regurgitating the same tired facts about our past successes or disappointments. We might even be connected with the past through old photos of unhappy years at school, or through old love letters from those who have long gone. The more we hold these things close, the more we live in the grip of the negative energies from the past.

In the great myths and tales those who take up the quest must always leave their homes and loved ones behind. As they depart they often perform the literal and symbolic act of shaking the dust from their cloak, because by leaving the past where it belongs they are better equipped to meet all the challenges in store for them. Sometimes they are even instructed not to look behind them – to do so would forfeit their ability to fulfil the quest. We too must learn to put the past firmly behind us.

The only real value the past holds for us is when it can enrich the present. As I continued to think about my student days, I realised I needed to gather up all the enthusiasm and vision I had enjoyed back then and re-inject it into my present life, then move on. As I did so, I felt happier and more relaxed than I'd felt in a long time.

Allowing the future to unfold

When we talk about uncluttering our lives, we aren't just talking about letting go of the things of the past. Equally we can find our selves trapped in the hope of an unrealistic future. Dream we must, but not all dreams are going to be realised. When we become so determined to get what we want, regardless of whether it is right for us, we miss out on the wider spectrum of life's possibilities. Of course we must aspire, but we must also have the courage to leave behind things that will never be.

I had always hoped to have children, but it never eventuated. In preparation for this happy event I had collected an exquisite range of toys and baby clothes. Yet even when it was clear there would be no child, I was unable to give away the drawers upon drawers of baby items. How could I, when I had pinned my hopes on having at least one child? When I finally came to terms with this, I realised that for me parenthood represented the ultimate act of creativity. Outside my work I had put my creativity on hold, waiting to invest it in my children. It was only when I had the courage to give the clothes and books and toys away that I was able to begin to embrace my creativity once more.

I had always had a head full of stories and one of my dreams had been to write, so I began to put pen to paper. My efforts culminated in getting a number of children's books and stories published. And when I talked with the children who read my tales, the satisfaction was immense. When I finally let go of something I was unable to have, the universe channelled me in a direction that satisfied not only my creativity but my deep love of children as well. This is the perfection of the universal plan. When we are amenable it then reveals to us the unique pattern of possibilities for all our lives.

Opening up to the universe

When this kind of fulfilment can be ours, why would we continue to cling to those aspects of our lives that are not working? The problem for most of us is that often we want to see how things are going to pan out before we commit our selves. Life doesn't always allow us to see the whole map, and so if we don't make a move we end up in a rut. This ability to trust the universe and move forward is not to abdicate responsibility for our lives, but to give us the courage we need to learn and to grow.

When we can relax a bit and go with the flow, then the universe will guide us accordingly. We will then get an inkling of what we should be up to. These inklings might come as feelings or dreams, or as chance remarks. How they come to us is less important than the fact that they *will* seek us out. And when we encounter them with an open mind, we are able to recognise them for what they are.

So as we seek to unclutter our lives, to free our selves from the limitations of living a purely material existence, we need to be aware of the movement of energy around us. In the natural course of things, energy flows uninterrupted. When, however, the energy around us becomes blocked, life's magic fades. If we hope to succeed on our quest we need to be vigilant so that always we keep life's energy moving around us and through us.

The joy of giving and receiving

As with so many universal laws, the law of giving and receiving is about balancing these energies. Many of us know how to give, but not how to receive. We delight in bestowing gifts on others, yet find it hard to allow others to do things for us. Often we put beautiful gifts away, waiting for the right moment to luxuriate in the warmth of someone else's kindness.

Some years ago I had to oversee the disposal of an elderly friend's effects. As I sorted through her possessions I was saddened to find her drawers were filled with exquisite possessions, many of which were still in their original wrappings. The pity wasn't that my friend hadn't surrounded herself with these things, but that perhaps her life might have been more joyous had she allowed either herself or others to enjoy some of the things she had locked away.

Similarly when we are constantly needy, when we feel we never have enough, where is the space to enjoy life's daily magic that already surrounds us? When we free our selves up from having to grasp at everything that comes our way, we attract those things that will transform our lives. Wonderful and beautiful things will then happen for us when we least expect it, making our lives an enchanting experience.

Being mindful of external pressures

In our quest to unclutter our lives we need to take great care not to become victims of external expectations, but to live within the present moment so that we can absorb all the riches available to us in the here and now.

I had a friend who lived in an old home on the fringe of the city. She enjoyed the wild overgrown garden that surrounded her house and the wonderful sense of community she shared with neighbours. As her career expanded, she began to fear her unfashionable location was at odds with her professional status. The more she thought about this, the more an inner-city location seemed the appropriate place to live. And so she moved into a city apartment.

Most of her furniture had to go, because it didn't fit her restricted space. She now lives at the 'right' address in incredibly cramped conditions with the constant grind of traffic outside. Although she hardly dares admit it, she misses her wild garden filled with its old trees. She misses the vine-laden pergola under which she shared many a memorable meal with family and friends. She still entertains, but there is a certain formality to her gatherings these days. Sadly her new home has done little to enhance her sense of worth. Rather she feels contained by it. It all seems so obvious when we view someone else's life, but how often do we compromise what we love for what we feel we should be doing or having?

Less is more

At the end of the day the ultimate question is how much does each of us need to be happy? Most of us aren't wealthy, but still we have many more things than we need. It is strange that at a time when we yearn for simplicity, we find our selves consuming more than ever before. In this time of great prosperity for some, the gap between those who have and those who have not continues to grow. Yet if we were to rid our selves of everything we didn't need, whether it be clothes, blankets, furniture or the mountains of food that lie idle, there would be less poverty, less hunger.

Recently a good friend spent some time amongst a group of native Americans. She was deeply moved by their way of life and their generosity. Not only did they make her welcome and feed and shelter her, but when she came to leave, they gave her some of their most treasured possessions without hesitation. They did this as an act of respect and love, because they inhabit an abundant universe. We, by contrast, have a great deal, but because we have no belief in the abundance of life we have little generosity of spirit.

In the end what we need most are those things that lift our hearts and feed our souls. If we can appreciate what we already have and make a practice of discarding as we accumulate and absorbing all that each moment brings, then we too will begin to taste the true lightness of being.

Uncluttering Our Lives

A prayer to help us unclutter

'O, Great Spirit, I have much in my life to be thankful for. Help me each and every day to make room to breathe and to allow new experiences to come to me. Help me also to be equally at home with giving and receiving. As I get rid of the clutter, may there be room in my life for all those precious things I need on my quest. And as I learn to live lightly, may all the good things that come to me bless my life and the lives of all living things.'

Attachment

Clinging to past wrongs

One of the greatest obstacles in our life's quest is attachment – the attachment we have not only to our possessions but to our beliefs and values. All of these things are a natural part of life, but unless they are kept in balance they will impede our progress.

All our attachments stem from what the Buddhists term the clinging mind – that aspect of our selves that is full of desire and that seizes on everything it sees without discernment. When our clinging mind is allowed to do what it wants, our many desires become those things we have to have or believe in. Then, before we realise it, they inform who we are and how we conduct our selves.

It is not until we begin to look at our notions that we see how easy it is to go along with attitudes and opinions that are not our own, that do not serve us well. Invariably those things we cling to narrow the view we hold of our selves and others. They encourage us to be self-seeking, and to say and do things that are ungenerous.

Often attachment creeps up on us unawares. When life has dealt us a hard blow it is tempting to revisit everything that has hurt us. The more we focus in on these things, the more our clinging mind will keep a catalogue of our woes, until we end up believing life isn't fair. And when we believe this, this is the energy we attract to us.

The great spiritual traditions encourage us to acknowledge everything that has been in our lives, then empty our selves of all those things that are no longer helpful so we can move on. When we can let go of all our limiting views and recollections, we can genuinely move into a new and better space. Then every time something hurtful reaches out to claim some part of us, we need to ask our selves whether or not we wish to allow it to do so. This is about learning to put things that disappoint to rest, so we can fully embrace all that each day has to offer us.

Letting go of our notions

If we allow it to, our clinging mind will influence our every belief. It will try to shape our notions of happiness even. It might well convince us that we must have a significant other or a new address if we want to be fulfilled, and unless we are aware of what is going on, we will run with the idea. All our precious life's energy and resources will be diverted into finding a new partner or new house. Then when we achieve this we cling to it believing our life's problems are solved.

The same thing happens when parents are so attached to their children they fail to give them the freedom they need to find their own way in life. Their love becomes suffocating and they will often end up driving their loved ones away. Similarly we can assume we are so indispensable at work that we make work our lives. Then we become dependent on our work to give our lives all the depth and meaning we crave. When we are in the grip of attachment, we fail to recognise where the source of our true nurture lies, and so we cling desperately to whatever love we have in our lives.

When we walk the path of the Sacred, however, we learn that the Great Spirit is our beloved. And when we open our selves up to this profound love, all other forms of love are merely reflections of this greater love. Then no longer do we need to measure out the love we give and receive. Still we cherish the love we have for others, but we hold this love lightly.

Ridding our selves of our fearfulness

The clinging mind will do all it can to prevent us from embracing our true selves, and fear is one of its most effective tools. Our fear makes us cling to what we know and understand, and if we do not take heart, our fearful notions will end up ruling our lives.

When we are feeling fearful it helps to ask our selves what the worst thing is that can happen to us if we move on from our fear, and then meditate on this question. If we make the time and space to do this, the fearful notions that have clouded our judgement will pass. We will then be able to see the situation with more clarity, and thus arrive at an appropriate answer.

While many of our fears are obvious, often our most deep-seated fears are not. When, however, we take the time to isolate what we fear most, we come to see what drives us. These are the fearful notions that rule our lives in unexpected ways. We then discover that because we are afraid we can never have a fulfilling relationship, we sabotage the good relationships we have had. Or because we fear for our children, we hold them so close they have little or no confidence in life.

Once we know what we are up against, we can do something about it. We might well need professional help, or we might feel able to move through these fears with the assistance of our sacred practices. Again our inner voice will serve us well in this regard. Then, as we move beyond the fears that bind us, we will be amazed how much more joyous our quest becomes.

Moving beyond the familiar

Our challenge is also to let go of attachment to the familiar, if it is just for attachment's sake: when we cling to the routine, we diminish the possibilities available to us. As we learn to live more lightly, we discover the joy that comes when we step outside the square. This isn't about turning our lives inside out, but about being a bit more adventurous about how we live our days. It is easy to slip into the same old way of doing things at home and at work, when our lives are so committed. Yet while we need structure in our lives, we need fun and new horizons as well. We might then be inspired to discover a different way home from work, a new course, or unusual foods we enjoy. No matter how insignificant the changes, they are worthwhile because they feed every part of us, encouraging us to live more creatively.

The importance of self-inquiry

As we become more aware of attachment in our lives, we can then make a habit of questioning what we do and why. Many notions we hold are not our own, but because they are ever present we adopt them without thinking. Some of these opinions have been formed by our friends and communities and some by our nationality even, but still we need to examine them closely, lest we find our selves supporting prejudices of the worst kind.

Always we must take care to consider the opinions that others would have us adopt and test them against our own in-sight. Some attitudes can seem harmless, yet still they can diminish our capacity to embrace life. In the West it is easy to assume that because our culture and values and ways of doing things work for us, ours is the only way to live. If we are not careful we can become smug about our technology and education, and end up clinging to a sense of superiority that deprives us of a more inclusive world view.

Watching out for our frustrations

Freeing our selves from our attachments includes learning to let go of all the little frustrations that end up eroding whatever joy there is in our days. Often when we awaken in the morning we are full of life. Then something happens to shatter our calm, and before we know it once more we are embroiled in those things that drag us down.

We lock horns with our boss, because her opinions differ from our own. We hear something about someone we dislike and immediately we assume it is fact and can't wait to tell others. Or we learn our workspace is being redesigned and immediately we are enraged and assume that we will be allotted a smaller space. These are just some of the many notions we encounter daily that threaten to overtake our wellbeing, our higher purpose.

Life beyond attachment

When we are trying to disengage from our attachments, we are best to begin with our sacred practice. As we become still, we start to become more conscious of the thoughts and situations that ambush us, then we can work to begin to control them before things get out of hand. We begin to see that even the most plausible arguments aren't necessarily for the benefit of everyone concerned, or we recognise the malicious comment carefully placed in the midst of an amusing conversation. When we are operating from a place of deep calm within, we start to become aware of our rigid notions that can erupt into frustrations, before they get out of hand. The more we do this, the easier life becomes.

Highly advanced souls have achieved greatness because they have mastered their need to be attached to people, to notions or to possessions. Their greatness lies in their being able to hold their place in the world lightly. They live with far greater freedom than most, yet in spite of this there is nothing in their ability to go with life's flow that is casual or careless. They too live and operate in the world and have worthwhile relationships but in the midst of this, always they strive to advance their life's quest. Because they are no longer weighed down by attachments, the code they live by is inspiring, and contagious – it encourages all those around them to achieve the extraordinary as well.

Each day as we continue to seek a more complete answer to the great question of life, 'Who Am I?', it becomes easier to catch the clinging mind at work. We are then able to ask our selves who is the 'I' that seeks to hold this opinion, to buy into this issue? And as we listen to our inner voice, we quickly discover that yet again our ego is attempting to live our lives for us. As we develop our awareness, instead of seizing on whatever is presented to us, we can choose carefully what we seek to carry with us. When we choose wisely, lightness of being will follow, allowing us to be true to our selves without fear or any sense of obligation.

A prayer to help us let go
'O, Great Spirit, as I enter this new day help me to see what thoughts and opinions I can do without. May I learn to love those in my life lightly, so that they too are free to pursue their

life's quest. Help me also to let go of anything else in my life that is no longer of benefit to me, so that each day I might travel lighter and with more purpose. And now as I seek to move beyond all those things that limit me, I give thanks for Your bounty, and pray that always my life will be a blessing to myself and to others.'

BUSYNESS

NO PAIN, NO GAIN
Time is one of our most precious commodities, not only because there is so little of it, but because our human lives are brief. We need to take care lest the many opportunities that come our way slip through our fingers, simply because we are too busy to appreciate them.

From our earliest years we are taught the need to strive and to work hard. We come to expect that life will be a challenge, and determined to prove our worth we start to run as hard and as fast as we can, and so the chronic busyness begins.

It is easy to get caught up in the endless rush of adrenaline – in wanting to be seen to be equal in every way to everyone around us. And why not? It is exhilarating to be out there making things happen. It feels good, it gets us noticed. And with all the effort we are putting into life, we assume we have got our act together. Yet when we step back from the madness and take a look at our lives, often we are dismayed to see they lack clarity, to see that our life's energy is being spent on things of little or no importance. In seeing this, we begin to understand why we feel so worn out most of the time.

All the chaos we battle daily has come about because we have lost our connection with the wisdom we carry deep inside. It is all too easy to confuse being busy with leading a purposeful life, but that's what most of us end up doing. Day in day out we run around from the moment we wake up, until we fling our selves back into bed late at night. The tragic thing is that in spite of all this effort, most of us can't even remember what we did last week, let alone what we did last month or the month before that. All we know is that we are exhausted. We dream of another way, but have no idea where we might find it. The busier we become the harder it is for us to see our way clear, because in spite of our many technological advances, in spite of all the seminars and books on time management and goal-setting, our lives continue to be frantic.

THE DEADENING EFFECT OF CHRONIC BUSYNESS

With this busyness comes an almost terminal exhaustion. We stop doing the things that make us happy and fulfilled. No longer do we take time to sit in the park, to walk by the sea, or to lighten and brighten our home or workplace. Then, before we know it, we have stopped putting effort into our meals and our health, until our lives are reduced to a daily ritual of convenience.

We yearn for a return to community, yet scarcely have our lives been more isolated. We long for tranquillity, yet our days are anything but tranquil. Each day we find our selves drifting a little further from our friends and family, until we are too busy and too tired to pick up the phone or to share a cup of coffee, because it will take time – time we don't seem to have. At the end of the day often we would rather slump in front of the TV than be with those we love, and when we do see friends, we feel as if we have little or nothing left to give.

Most of us have tried to get our chronic busyness under control. We have attempted to claw back our lives, but with little effect. The problem is that when we try to change our lives we tend to focus on externals. We attempt to organise our selves and others better. This might help, but no matter how organised we are, we cannot arrest the madness that surrounds us. Sooner or later we will find our selves giving in to these pressures.

Recognising our ego at work

The secret to being able to move beyond all this activity is to discover that sacred place inside us that is untouched by busyness. Here is where all the peace and nurture reside. Here also is the perspective we so desperately need.

Once we find this place we are able to see what lies *behind* our need to be constantly on the go. We then see that we have been afraid to say no, lest we be lonely or be seen as a loser. Then, as we go deeper still, we recognise that our chronic busyness is merely the prompting of our ego. This is what causes us to flog our selves to death. This is what stands between us and our freedom.

Moving beyond the busyness

Those who have achieved the extraordinary have done so by stepping beyond the expectations of others, and we must do the same. We begin our journey beyond busyness, when we can put space between us and the rest of the world, when we can allow our selves the time to think and to be, and when we can access that space beyond our many thoughts. Contrary to what we might fear, we don't cease to exist, but we do get a life.

As we seek more balance, again we come back to the importance of meditation and of moments of quiet through the day. When we find time to be still, we have the opportunity to shed all the petty hurts and annoyances we have absorbed, before they become part of us.

When we access this space beyond busyness, life comes into sharp focus. Solutions to problems are made apparent to us. We become inspired about a new project. We are reminded of a friend who needs the warmth of our company. We might only be able to snatch five minutes' space here and there in the day, but as we become used to switching off, we will find that time will slow, allowing us to get through all the things we need to, without the gut-wrenching anxiety we are so familiar with.

When we begin to experience this level of calm, we can further enhance this experience by consciously inviting peace and love and joy into every cell in our body. As these elements enter our being, we will feel them further transforming us as our bodies fill with Light. We start to enjoy this all-encompassing calm, and find our selves creating even more opportunities for stillness.

Embracing the piquancy of everyday living

This new way of living brings many gifts. It enables us to look deeply into all that is around us. So when we observe a rose, for example, we learn to see it more fully, to lose our selves in the intensity of its colour, in the fragile beauty of its petals, in its subtle fragrance. And as we do so, we find our selves able to go deeper still. We then touch the singular life of this flower. We marvel at the fact it is every bit as alive as we are, and that it too has struggled to grow and thrive, to reach its fruition. No rose that has bloomed on Earth or is yet to bloom will be the same as this flower before us. And as we honour this unique life, we become aware that this moment will never come again. This, we realise, is the nature of every single moment of our lives. Inspired, we are then able to gather up all the beauty and in-sight this moment offers.

This is what the sacred magic of human life is all about. As we begin to appreciate all living things, we experience what it is like to be one with the world around us. Imagine being able to live each moment with this level of oneness and awe. This is the world that awaits us beyond the busyness, and the more we shed our need to fill every moment with activity, the more we will experience what it is like to come home to our sacred selves.

In his exquisite work, *Anam Cara: A Book of Celtic Wisdom*, John O'Donohue informs us that the Celts believed our bodies were cocooned *within* the soul. This is a beautiful possibility, is it not? It gives us a real sense of how profound life can be when we allow our selves to be swathed in the Sacred, to be cloaked in our divinity. We get an inkling of how this feels when we are on holiday or when we can simply be. In these rare moments every part of our being soars, as we experience the freedom that comes when we empty our selves of all that we carry daily. This is what is meant by lightness of being. This is the deep joy that can be ours, not just in our quiet moments or in our special places, but each and every moment of the day.

When we leave our freneticism behind our every experience is heightened, as is our sense of discovery. When we become still, we tread the realms of the Sacred, and there we discover all the wisdom and in-sight we could hope for. As the stillness becomes our friend, we move beyond the need to make life a big production. When we have nothing to prove, we are able to allow love to inspire and inform all we do. We then think before we speak. We act with more foresight as well, because we are now able to sense what is worthy of our life's energy and what is not.

So precious do these moments of stillness become that we find our selves more creative about how we invite stillness into our everyday lives. So instead of reading a magazine or a paper while commuting to and from work, we might choose to gaze out of the window and observe the sky and the trees. As we tread the pavements of our busy city streets, we might then hold onto this stillness by remembering to give thanks for the air we breathe, for our food and clothing and for all that is available to us.

BEING IS DOING

Our journey beyond the busyness isn't about retiring from life so much as learning to operate effectively within it. This means dealing with the freneticism rather than simply trying to avoid it. We do this by recognising there are times for action and times for stillness. Again we are brought back to the law of balance, or, as the Buddhists would describe it, the middle way.

There is more to stillness than becoming calm. So caught up can we become in proving ourselves, in being 'out there', that we don't realise that being *who* we are is more powerful than anything we might say or do. We all know when we are in the presence of great goodness and love – we sense it immediately. We only have to catch sight of the people who embody these qualities and at once we are filled with joy and immense hopefulness. This is the power of being, and the more we allow the Light to infuse us, the more we are able to shed Light on those around us and to encourage them in their own quest towards lightness of being.

It is in our moments of stillness that we make contact with the Source of All Being, with that which sustains us and always will. And it is in these moments that we receive the strength and stability needed to meet life's many challenges. None of this is difficult, not if we are mindful. But to be mindful we need also to be vigilant, because living as we do in a time of enormous change it is easy to become distracted.

Reclaiming those parts of our selves that have become scattered

The journey through earthly life is designed to take us beyond illusion to those things of permanence that lie beyond the limits of time and space. So part of life's quest is about learning to deal with life's frenzy.

Even though daily life is constantly changing, we learn to guard our life's energy with great care. When we stop squandering our time and energy and creativity on the things that don't matter, we are able to gather up all the disparate parts of our selves that we have given away, knowing that we can only make the most of our beautiful, unique lives when we retrieve all those parts of us that we had lost. Then when we are whole we are able to move forward, more alive than ever before.

Learning to deal with one thing at a time

Learning to deal with one thing at a time doesn't mean that we will never have a lot on our plate. Still there will be times when our tasks are many and our resources few.

When this happens, we simply do one thing at a time and hand the rest back to God. This means that we need to be wise enough to recognise what we are capable of and what is beyond us at any moment in time. When we do genuinely hand back the details of our lives to the Source of All Things, whatever we need will be accomplished with ease.

Part of our journey towards self-fulfilment is a journey towards effortlessness, and this effortlessness is to be found beyond the busyness. When we let go the busyness there lies all the ease and joy and beauty we could hope for.

A prayer on becoming still

'O, Great Spirit, help me to remember that what I am is of far greater importance than what I do. Help me to recognise also that nothing is more important than my wellbeing, because the more whole I am, the further I am able to travel on my life's quest.

'In the stillness of each day help me to shed all those things that do not serve my life's purpose, so that I too can gain lightness of being. In all the activities I undertake, help me to go about my tasks with love and in-sight, so that I can infuse the dark places in life with the Light of the Sacred.

'And when I'm feeling overwhelmed or fearful, help me to simply deal with what is immediately in front of me and to hand the rest back to You, knowing that the rest is not my problem.

'Thank you for this day of my life and for all the opportunities it will bring.'

THE PATH OF HARMLESSNESS

THE PRACTICE OF HARMLESSNESS BEGINS DEEP WITHIN

When we think about harmlessness it is easy to assume we don't need to give it much thought. Already we care about the planet, about children having enough food to eat and about keeping our streets safe. Yet while this is commendable, the path of harmlessness encompasses a great deal more than this.

True harmlessness informs our every thought and action. It honours the miracle of life and the interconnectedness of all things. And so whether we are a snail or a snow leopard or a Mexican farmer, we all hold our life dear. We all seek to thrive and be happy. When we understand how precious life is to each living thing, no longer can we be careless about anything that exists. We are then inspired to do our utmost to ensure we will never harm another. And when we are able to live this way, no one has anything to fear from us.

The path of harmlessness is central to our life's quest, because we are here to expand our soul awareness. As we embrace harmlessness, we learn to break through the crust of our limited perceptions so that we too can become wiser and more able to love.

We can only honour the lives of others when we are able to honour our own lives. We have talked already about the need to be gentle on our selves, but if we are to be truly harmless we must do a great deal more than this. We must take responsibility for every aspect of our lives, from the energy we inhabit to the food we eat and the company we keep.

Every part of our being is precious, because it is the dwelling place of our spirit. It not only needs rest and nurture, but time for in-sight and contemplation, and for fun and laughter as well. We cannot embrace the world around us, if we are not at peace within. Too often we neglect our selves. We don't eat well, we don't surround our selves with people and situations that uplift us. Then, as exhaustion or depression take hold, we resort to distractions that dull our perceptions, that create dependency.

Even the way we choose to express our selves sexually is often harmful to our selves and others. For many, sex has little meaning, let alone any sense of responsibility. So lost are many within their preconceptions about relationships that they have no sense of what it means to genuinely love another. If we wish to live harmlessly we cannot harm others, nor can we allow others to harm us. We weren't put on Earth to abuse or be abused.

Learning to love

When we are able to tread the path of harmlessness we will reach a quality of love that will often astonish our selves and others. We will find that people will want to be with us, because they feel safe and energised and uplifted, because of who we are deep within our being.

When we create a safe space around us we give others the freedom to laugh and cry with us, to face birth and death with us. And in sharing these experiences, we too will touch the extraordinary beauty at the heart of the human quest.

Our capacity to live harmlessly is limited only by our imaginations

The path of harmlessness is all-embracing. It can even inform the way we dress. There has been much talk about dressing for success, when what we are really talking about is presenting our selves aggressively to the world, getting our selves noticed no matter what. Imagine how different our days might be if we were to dress with gentleness and beauty, if we were to dress to make our souls sing. This holds true not just for clothes but for all that we seek to gather around us, whether it be people or pastimes or possessions.

Honouring nature

When we take the path of harmlessness seriously we become far more aware of all the resources we have access to, and of how few resources most of the world exists on. As we reflect on this, our neediness dissolves. We then find we are no longer driven to have more than we need. If anything we find our selves yearning to travel lighter still, so that we can move with ease wherever life takes us.

Then we begin to care about what we clean our homes with, as much as we care about preserving the wilderness and all the creatures that seek to thrive there. We learn to respect the many creatures we encounter as well. I had a teacher who used to rescue stranded worms from wet pavements. Seeing this I was also inspired to rescue worms, and from this simple act I then became aware of how many other creatures could benefit from a little loving-kindness and consideration.

Embracing harmlessness no matter what

There will be times when we have to make decisions that have the potential to hurt others. When we are in this place, we need all the determination we can muster to continue to hold the Light. So instead of wanting to hit out or to even the score, we learn to call on the sustenance we need to enable us to rise above all the pain and emotion, aware that we cannot add to the darkness of ignorance and suffering in any way. This does not mean that we condone evil, but that we recognise we are here to enhance the Light. This can be challenging, yet when we become still we will gain the in-sight we need to deal with the situation in as compassionate a way as possible.

When a dear friend realised her marriage of years was at an end, her natural impulse was to leave the relationship as soon as possible. Her husband wasn't a terrible man, but they had been strangers for a long time. Following the promptings of her inner voice, she ended up taking the process more slowly. As she made her intentions clear, she took great pains to emphasise the fact that she still loved and valued her husband, and that she would be there for him in the future. There were painful times and many tears, but there was also a lot of joy. They even went apartment hunting together, determined to find the right living space for each other. After they separated they saw one another regularly, and continued to care for each other whenever one of them was sick.

While this level of caring is not always possible, particularly if one is leaving an abusive situation, what helped my friend was that she prayed repeatedly to the Great Spirit, asking that their situation be filled with Light and Love, thus ensuring the best outcome for them both. The years since their divorce have not been without challenge, but they now both find themselves in circumstances that are absolutely right for them. This is the magic of treading lightly and harmlessly through life.

Dealing with life's little lacerations

Often what catches us out on the path of harmlessness are the daily frustrations that get under our skin. So caught up can we find our selves in the business of living that it becomes hard for us to project our selves beyond what is immediately ahead. When something happens that we don't like, we simply react. Then something else takes place and we react to that as well, and before we know it, ours has become a roller-coaster way of living.

On the days we are at the top of the roller-coaster, we feel as if no one can test our goodwill, but on the days that challenge us we have little room in our hearts to be even-handed. It is on the difficult days when the careless remark or the thoughtless gesture can wound us so, and because we have become so used to reacting, we rise to the bait and end up saying and doing things we regret. We know we are meant to live harmlessly, and we really do want to live harmlessly, yet all we can think of is how we can retaliate. Then when the dust settles we wonder why we allow certain people to get to us. We know it's not the way to live and we resolve not to let things bother us, and thus life goes on in a never-ending cycle of conflict and resolution. When we live harmlessly we learn to be more discerning and to move beyond the ego – beyond the need to always be right and to prove our selves at the expense of others.

Gaining control of our thoughts

Harmlessness encompasses our thoughts. This is not something we are likely to achieve overnight, but achieve it we must. When we catch our selves thinking unworthy thoughts we are best to observe them and let them go. To explore them is to invite their dark energies in. It doesn't hurt to remind our selves that every unworthy thought detracts from who we are in essence. By the same token, every positive thought and intention we have enhances the Light, and draws heaven and Earth closer.

Might is not right

Often our difficulties in living harmlessly are not to do with our willingness to change, but with our fears that if we take the path of peace we will make our selves vulnerable to all the negative influences around us. In a world that is as aggressive as ours, it is easy to see harmlessness as weakness. Nothing, however, could be further from the truth. We need only look at the lives of Gandhi and Mandela to understand the awesome power of goodness.

Harmlessness empowers who we are at every level of our being. It enables us to live as we were intended to, wholly and fully, beyond the many fears that seek to imprison us with self-doubt or despair. Once we grasp this, no longer do we have to be defensive or aggressive when things don't go our way, because we are reminded that the universe is a loving and sustaining space, and that everything is unfolding as it should. When we know where our guidance and sustenance lie, then we have no need of quick-fix solutions. Instead we are able to remain consistent in all that we do.

Becoming aligned to our higher purpose

It is easy to embrace harmlessness as an ideal. When, however, we meet questionable behaviour, we need to summon all the

The Path of Harmlessness

courage and in-sight we can, so we can move forward without fear or favour. When these situations arise, they require us to be clear about our ethics. If it is appropriate to speak out, we must speak our truth simply and with conviction, because it is the intention we apply to contentious issues that is vital. Sometimes words and deeds will not help, so in situations such as this we serve our selves and others best by holding firmly to a good outcome for all concerned.

At one stage I was in a two-day business negotiation, which had the potential to get ugly. People's jobs were on the line, and so it wasn't exactly the happiest of scenarios.

Each day before the meeting started I prayed that the outcome would be for the highest good of all those involved, and every time I felt myself or others becoming frustrated I would remind myself of this intention.

Having sought this I then had to be open to the solutions that presented themselves. Not only did I make a major shift from my intended stance, but so did my colleagues. In the end the solution we arrived at not only utilised everyone's strengths, but it was absolutely fair as well. Always the path of harmlessness is practical and wise, and whatever gains are made are never at the expense of others.

When we seek to live harmlessly we discover what really sustains us. And so even when life has its disappointments, we are able to let go of our hurts more easily, because we don't want anything to stand between us and the deep joy we experience when we tread lightly and mindfully. The path of harmlessness will not fail us. It leads us to a peace that surpasses our normal understanding, as daily we stretch our capacity to love and to become wise.

A prayer on being harmless

'O, Great Spirit, as I honour each and every day of my life, help me also to honour the lives of those around me. Help me to deal wisely and lovingly with all I meet, so that at the end of each day this planet is a little better than I found it. Help me never to give in to those things that take from the Light and the Love I carry within. Give me the courage to be my best self in good times and bad, and to help others to do likewise, so that always we light the way for each other.'

THE GIFT OF FORGIVENESS

THE ALCHEMY OF FORGIVENESS

Sorry is probably the hardest word to say in any language and yet it is the word that can and does change lives, that mends friendships and families, that makes the future a far more promising space. Most of us know this already, yet in spite of this forgiveness doesn't come easily, because it takes us out of our comfort zone.

When we fail to rectify a situation and move on, not only do we perpetuate all the dark energies we seek to escape, we absorb them as well. Then, instead of being able to look beyond our discomfort, we replay what has happened over and over, losing all perspective, until what began as an unfortunate remark or action becomes something larger. And the more we give in to our anger and hurt, the more all the positive energy we have gained through our sacred practices and through our attempts to lead a decent life is eroded.

We will always know when the lighter energies we have attained are slipping away from us, because we will feel lost and confused. When we are in this state of mind we cannot deal wisely and compassionately with difficult situations, let alone move beyond them.

Forgiveness is an alchemy of sorts that enables us to transform all the dark energies in our lives into those that are infused with Light. Instead of being defeated by our disappointments, we allow all negative energies to flow past us, so that always our personal space remains a sacred one.

When we operate from a sacred space, we are able to see beyond the unhelpful remark into the heart of whatever conflict is before us. By living in a space of absolute integrity and concentrating on setting things right, we create a positive space not only for our selves, but for all involved. This, in turn, makes it easier for everyone to be part of the forgiveness process.

FORGIVENESS IS SIMPLY ANOTHER FORM OF HEALING

When we are able to turn our dark moments into Light, we are able to use every situation in our lives to invite more Light in. Then not only will life hold less conflict, we will feel the profound effect of this enlightening process on every level of our being. Ridding our selves of all the petty details and unhelpful energies in our lives and healing what needs healing gives us the space to savour life and to appreciate its many rich and beautiful textures.

Already most of us are able to find the room in our hearts to forgive. Sometimes it seems as if we are always forgiving, yet when we begin to look at the people we forgive, we realise that more often than not our compassion only extends as far as those we care about. It is good that we can forgive, because not only do we have the opportunity to stretch our capacity to love, we invite into our being the very energies that nurture our souls. Then, as we continue to enhance our sacred space, not only are we better equipped to deal with trying people and situations, we are able to use our vitality for things that matter.

Finding the freedom to forgive

As we consider the possibilities for forgiveness we need to be aware of the space in which we live. Do we inhabit a space that is Light and loving, that allows others to feel free to admit their errors, or have we become so far removed from these energies that even if someone were to apologise we would be unlikely to be gracious? Does our energy allow us the freedom to confess our own shortcomings, or are we so lost in our anxieties and in how others see us that self-forgiveness is out of the question?

Most of us do want to forgive or be forgiven. We do want to put unfortunate incidents behind us, yet often there is some part of us that can't quite relent, that clings to our anger and despair. As we look more closely at these emotions, we see that this part of us is afraid to be wrong or to deal with confronting situations. And as we examine this fear, we begin to see how it affects our dealings with others. We see where it makes us defensive, inflexible or confrontational even. Then we realise that this is the energy that makes our lives and the lives of those around us an uncomfortable space. We can also see that the more conflict we draw to us, the harder it becomes to let love and compassion in.

When we allow our lives to be fearful, we stop seeing all the possibilities that are there for us. When we cling to the way we think life should be, we don't realise that it is the ability to let go a little and to lighten up that enables us to free our selves and others from all the guilt and recrimination that sticks to us when things go wrong.

Moving beyond our fears and anxieties

Whenever we consider the possibility of forgiveness always we must do so lightly. All that is asked of us is that we set the healing power of forgiveness in motion, and then allow life's wider pattern to reveal itself. This means letting go of our own preconceived ideas of how a situation will resolve itself.

Often we limit the possibilities for forgiveness with our notions of how certain issues should be played out. We see former lovers gathering us up in their arms with promises of undying devotion, or we imagine our work mates treating us like heroes. These kinds of fantasies might delight our ego, but this is not what forgiveness is about. True forgiveness is about healing a difficult situation, then moving on.

The art of letting go

Forgiveness is about freeing our selves from situations that limit us, not about punishment. It is, however, an art that can challenge even the best of us. This is beautifully illustrated in a story of two monks standing by a river who were joined by a young woman. As they stood before the swift-flowing water it became clear that the young stranger would never reach the other side without assistance, and so one of the monks offered to carry her. Relieved, the young woman accepted and off they set. When they reached the far bank the young woman was set down and went on her way. As the monks continued on their journey, they did so in strained silence. After they had gone some distance, the monk who had assisted the young woman across the river paused. 'If I was able to leave the young woman behind when we crossed the river, why can't you?' he asked his companion. Which of the two monks are we? Do we cling to the past and to our preconceptions of how things should be, or are we able to move on from circumstances that surprise or disturb us?

Forgiveness comes into our lives to stretch our understanding of who we are and who we yet might be. And as we become more at home with the practice of letting go of past hurts and mistakes, the more it will become a way of life.

Ensuring the past is well and truly behind us

There will be times when we think we are over something, only to find the past returning to haunt us. When this happens it is nothing to be alarmed about. These situations come to us to help us practise our resolve. All we need do is observe the energy behind the issue concerned, then gently but firmly let it go.

If the thoughts and details surrounding the situation persist, it helps to find some time to be still. Once in this place of stillness we can visualise our selves being surrounded and suffused with Light. Then we can anchor our selves in our divine centre by repeating, 'I AM Light'. As we continue to repeat this phrase we bring our selves back to balance by reminding our selves who we really are.

When the past returns to greet us, it is useful to examine what is going on in our lives at present. Often we will discover the issues or emotions from our past are mirroring what is going on in our lives right now. Again this is nothing to worry about, because once we are aware that certain aspects of our lives need help, we can set about healing them.

Josh had spent a number of years wrestling with an addiction that arose from the use of prescription drugs after an operation. When his addiction was at its worst he did many unfortunate things. In the years since then he has led a good and fruitful life. Occasionally, unpleasant incidents from the past come back to haunt him. Josh now realises that this happens when he is overtired, or when his self-esteem has taken a dive. While Josh would prefer the past remain where it belongs, he now finds it a useful barometer to take a good look at his life right now and see where his self-esteem needs some nurturing at present. By doing so he is using the darkness in his past to light his way forward.

When we choose to forgive our selves and others and set our selves free from the past, we must do so authentically and humbly and wholeheartedly, and then leave the issue behind. Once something is healed, what is past must remain in the past. We cannot say we have forgiven someone and still think they are an idiot or that they are not to be trusted. Once we have forgiven we must endeavour not to comment or think about them negatively either, because every time we do so we allow our anger and despair to grow.

Finding the courage to face unresolved issues

There are times when we do want to forgive, but we are afraid of how others will react, and so we delay the opportunity for forgiveness, not realising that when we delay we achieve nothing. Unresolved issues are like wounds that fail to heal. We can ignore our woundedness as long as we like, but it won't go away.

Forgiveness brings great gifts, but it requires courage also. We still have to face the possibility that things might not be resolved in the way we would hope. So while we forgive someone else, they won't necessarily forgive us. This can seem discouraging, but only when we forget the true purpose of forgiveness is to heal what needs healing. When we move beyond being a victim, we free our selves of whatever is holding us back, whether or not others come to the party, then we can get on with the business of living.

At one stage Alberto was cut loose by his parents, because they didn't approve of his partner. Although he was living in San Diego and his parents were in South Africa, he felt their rejection keenly. Every week he would drop his parents a note or send them a gift, because he never wanted his parents to worry about him. Time passed but still his carefully chosen presents were returned. Letters would remain unanswered and Alberto was close to despair. He would often wake in the night and pray for reconciliation, but the outright rejection continued, until he finally realised there was nothing more he could do. All the will in the world, all the positive thinking wasn't going to change his parents' attitude.

After allowing the constant pain of rejection to blight his life for a couple of years, Alberto realised he needed to let go of his desire to have his parents acknowledge him. When he was able to do this, he discovered that what he was left with was the desire to be loving towards his parents simply for the sake of being loving. And so these days when he writes his weekly letters home, he does so purely as an act of love.

While Alberto has never had the joy of being accepted by his parents, he now enjoys the deep soul satisfaction that comes when we embrace the path of goodness for goodness' sake. Through this heart-rending situation Alberto has benefited greatly, because he has learned the power of grace, and as he has let go of his hurt, his life has deepened immeasurably.

Forgiveness in and around death

Sometimes we yearn to be able to give or gain forgiveness from those who are no longer with us, but because they have died we assume that these matters will never be resolved. Often we live with the pain of this for years, not realising there is nowhere in the universe that is beyond the healing light of forgiveness. Death is merely a doorway to another dimension of being, so just because we can no longer sit down and have a chat or ring each other up, it doesn't mean we can't resolve matters needing forgiveness. The miracle is that the healing power of forgiveness reaches beyond the boundaries of countries, beyond time and space even.

A number of years ago Chloe admitted to having been badly treated as a small child. By the time she was ready to forgive, those who had harmed her had all passed away. Although Chloe knew she was unlikely to forget her suffering, she wanted to let go of all the negative emotion that surrounded those years. After making time to forgive those concerned with a short prayer, Chloe bought a lilac tree and planted it in her front garden. Now whenever she pauses to enjoy its distinctive flowers and its heady scent, her heart is filled with the immense peace that comes when we let go of our past.

When we wish to forgive or to gain forgiveness from those who have passed over, it helps to set aside time to be still. Again this is a sacred moment and so we should begin by blessing the space. We might even wish to light a candle or to burn an essential oil. As we relax we can visualise everyone involved in this healing being swathed in the beauty of Divine Light. When we are enclosed in this space, we can lovingly state what needs to be said. This can be done as a prayer or as a conversation, either spoken out loud or to our selves. If there are a number of people involved, it is best to address each one in turn. Once we are done we can bless and honour all concerned, asking that they be released to their highest good. Then, as we give thanks to the Great Spirit, we can let go of all that has burdened us and move on. We might even light a candle for them now and again, to bless them on the next stage of the journey.

As we gain greater in-sight into the possibilities that forgiveness presents us, the more we are able to gather up our despair and disappointments, and transform them into something beautiful. This is what the great souls have always done. This is what those who feed the hungry, who nurse the sick and who care for the dying do every day of the week. We can do these kinds of things in ways that are meaningful and appropriate as well.

Daring to forgive our selves

Often it is finding the capacity to forgive our selves that we wrestle with most. So relentless are we with blaming our selves that we end up weighed down with guilt. Yet when we are unforgiving towards our selves we achieve little, because we diminish our sacred potential. And when we can't forgive our selves, how can we be genuinely more understanding of others?

It is easy to beat our selves up about our many mistakes, but we must never forget that they provide us with valuable soul learning. We are here because we are all works in progress, and so even when we have made a mess of things, there is no point in collapsing in recrimination or despair. We too need compassion. We too need the opportunity to make each day a new and glorious creation. Always we must recognise those things we have done badly and seek to redress them, then move forward. There is no point in remaining lost in blame and shame.

If we are able to embrace life's sacred alchemy, even the difficult things that come our way can prove to be our greatest friends. When we understand this, nothing that happens to us need ever be lost. And so when we make mistakes, if we deal with them positively we are able to learn and grow. Even those in spirit are able to observe us. Believe it or not our triumphs and failures assist them with their soul learning as well.

So often the things that haunt us are fed by our own lack of self-worth. This is not helpful, because every time we lose a sense of who we are, we deny our divinity and all the wisdom and in-sight it brings to our lives. We have all done things we regret, and given the chance there is no way we would do these things again. We cannot change our past, but we can heal it.

When we have taken a wrong turn we need the healing power of love more than ever, because it is through love that we are able to become whole. When we have all the love we need, then even when things go wrong we are able to move forward in search of a solution, because we naturally seek to forgive rather than condemn.

No one is beyond forgiveness

When we choose to incarnate we carry with us a great responsibility, because each day we are either adding to the Light of the world or we are diminishing it. There is nothing in between. When we can remain centred in who we are, we are able to let the folly of the moment pass. We then recognise that while we cannot solve all the problems of this planet of ours, we can assist humanity by rising above the need to judge and by healing the dark places wherever we can, because no one is beyond the immense power and compassion of the Light.

A few years ago I came across a young woman whose misdemeanours had landed her in a high-security prison. Someone had taken a contract out on her life, and while she was in prison she was stabbed. As the blade sliced her flesh she was catapulted out of her body and into the Light. There she met angelic beings, who lovingly made her shortcomings clear to her. She was then given the opportunity to return to Earth and amend her ways. The moment she agreed to do so, she was back in her body and being rushed to hospital. So profound was this experience that her life was transformed from that moment. She served her time and now lives a decent and fruitful life.

Who would have guessed at this person's potential? But there it was, simply waiting for the right catalyst to allow it to unfold. Of course we need laws and those who transgress must be dealt with, but it doesn't serve us well when we seek to be judge, jury and executioner. Buddhist teachings challenge us to seek good outcomes for all, including those who do us wrong.

Our essential natures are not only made of Light, they are made of Love also, and every part of our being thrives when we are loving. Sooner or later we will discover the immense scope of Divine Love – when we experience this for our selves we will know with absolute certainty that the love of the Great Spirit is ours in life's exquisite moments and in the desperate moments as well. So even though there might be times when we are driven to the very edge of the abyss, we can draw strength from the fact that the universe will never forsake us. Always we will be given the sustenance we need, and the more we access this sustenance, the safer our world will become.

A meditation on forgiveness

Find yourself a place where you can be still, and as you settle allow your attention to return to your body. Then, as you become aware of the steady flow of your breath, allow every part of your body, including your shoulders and the many muscles around your face, to relax.

Now, as you leave the everyday world behind, let your mind become still. Where any thoughts arise, simply let them pass. Then, as you relax in the stillness, take a moment to invite the Great Spirit to be present with you in this healing moment. Feel the energy of the Divine Presence draw close and allow yourself to become one with this love, until you too become this perfect love.

Then, as you linger in the absolute beauty of this boundless love, you now recall the hurt that you seek to heal. As you do so, you move past this hurt to look more deeply within. Here for one precious moment you are privileged to observe yourself at your most sacred. By experiencing the sheer magnitude of your divine self, you realise that you are much greater, much more profound, than this hurt before you.

In this moment you recognise that this is your centre of power and in-sight and wisdom. Let yourself take in this completeness and see that when you operate without this knowledge, you feel a sense that something is lacking. You see also that it is this lack that creates all the confusion and conflict in your life. As you acknowledge this, take a moment to become intimate with the sacred dimensions of your existence.

Now, as you slowly turn your attention to the person with whom you have certain issues, see this person standing before you in your mind's eye. Observe them as if you were seeing them for the very first time. Become aware of the energy that surrounds them. Note their stance, the expression on their face, the look in their eyes. See them as you have never seen them before.

You see they lack many of the things that bless your life. You realise that this person has their own fragilities and anxieties, with which they battle. While observing this, feel the energy between you softening as you are reminded that they too are works in progress. Then, as you go deeper still, you see that they have that within which is Divine, which connects them with all living things. And as you honour this, you realise that at the most fundamental level of existence you are one.

Now, as you acknowledge the sacred link between you, make amends for anything that has been said or done that has caused pain or misfortune. As you seek the healing power of forgiveness, feel the light of truth surrounding and suffusing you both, as all the hurt that has existed between you drops away. Feel the absolute relief of it throughout your whole being. And as all the hurt that exists between you dissolves, allow the space between you to be filled with Light. When the forgiveness is complete, hold this healing energy close.

Then, before you return to the everyday world, take a moment to thank the Great Spirit for freeing you from this situation, in your own words or as follows:

'O, Great Spirit, I honour Your Sacred Presence in this healing moment. My heart fills to see all the unhappiness that has existed between us transformed into the Pure Light of Your Being. From this day on may our lives reflect this Divine Light in all that we do and think and say. May our days be blessed with Your Peace and Joy and Love, and may we walk in the path of goodness and truth from this day on.'

As you open your eyes, take a moment to reflect on all that has taken place here. And as you return to everyday life, may you walk in beauty and in peace. May all that you have learned from this experience enhance your compassion. May it assist you greatly on your quest to become wise.

Transforming Our Work

The challenge of work

Work can be one of our life's many passions or it can be our daily descent into hell. Today work looms so large in our lives that it is easy to allow it to consume us body and soul. When work is going well we are on cloud nine, but when it isn't delivering all we had hoped for we are traumatised.

Work can be one of our life's greatest challenges, because it is here that we witness the best and worst of our selves and others. It is here where the goal posts change constantly, as does the balance of power, where everything we believe in and everything we stand for can be tested to the limit.

If we have any hope of dealing with work, we need to know how to anchor our selves firmly in all that is sacred. We do this by honouring our sacred practices, by being clear about our values, and by knowing what sustains us and what doesn't. If we don't have an intimate relationship with the Divine, whenever work gets tricky we are likely to be thrown off course. We will then find our selves obsessing about our work and our work mates, and clinging to every detail.

When it gets too much, we dream about abandoning our day

job and taking our selves off to a deserted spot where we can just be. Or we fantasise about working in a stimulating environment surrounded by like-minded people. We might even be tempted to join a religious order, or to live alone on a mountain top where we can have some peace, and can be the person we want to be.

WE TAKE OUR SELVES WITH US WHEREVER WE GO

Most of us don't have the option of handing in our resignation, and even if we did, still we would carry our baggage with us. No matter where we are, sooner or later the lessons we are grappling with will follow. Work life will always have its moments, but it is also an invaluable arena in which to learn the lessons we need to learn. Then, instead of battling the same issues over and over, we can begin to isolate those things that are holding us back, and heal them once and for all.

As well as paying the rent and putting food on the table, work gives us many chances to connect with our own sacred possibilities, because it is in this hothouse of ambitions and political manoeuvring that we have the perfect chance to explore more deeply all that it means to be human.

KNOWING WHEN TO STAY

When things aren't going well it is easy to lose patience and to seek another job in the hope of a quick way out. This might be the right course of action, but equally we might not have learnt all the lessons our current workplace has to teach us. By moving on prematurely we might miss out on all the blessings that would be ours if we have the courage to ride out the storm and see what lies beyond it.

We can only discover the depth and breadth of what we are capable of when our resources are put to the test. We refine these resources in the same way an athlete builds their stamina — by placing our selves in situations that enhance who we are. And so when we are feeling unhappy or generally disaffected, it is important to move past our thoughts and emotions and go deep inside, so we can see what in-sight is there for us.

A good friend, Julian, had a boss who treated his staff poorly. Always Julian tried to remain respectful and dignified in the face of constant sarcasm and mean-spirited behaviour. Those who valued Julian often wondered why he didn't simply resign, because he had the talent and the track record to get another job without any trouble, but Julian was adamant he was where he was meant to be. This was the guidance he had received.

In spite of constant discouragement, Julian continued to support and nurture those around him and to be exceptional at all he did. Over time he reached a state where he was greatly blessed, because in amongst the difficulties he had to face, Julian discovered the source of his strength, his self-esteem and his love of life. Not only did Julian benefit from this deep soul learning, his career progressed beyond all expectations as well.

In the end Julian was deeply grateful to his difficult boss, because it was his active discouragement that strengthened Julian's sense of purpose at work and in his spiritual life as well. In spite of everything, Julian's boss had been one of his greatest catalysts for positive change, and Julian ended up feeling fulfilled in every aspect of his life. When we can move beyond our emotional responses to life's challenging situations, to those in work life in particular, often a whole new spectrum of opportunities awaits us.

As we progress we realise that the inner and outer worlds are inextricably linked, and that as we heal the issues around our work, we heal our selves also. Then, as we learn to balance our inner and outer worlds, no longer are we locked into narrow definitions and expectations of who we imagine our selves to be. Even though we might gain great fulfilment from work, we know that we are far greater than anything we might achieve in our careers.

Whether we are a typist or a brain surgeon, a prime minister or a palaeontologist is of little interest to the Great Spirit. What matters is how we conduct our selves. Always we must perform our work to the very best of our ability. We must be decent and diligent and focused and trustworthy in all that we say and do. Then our sacred path becomes a living path and not just a set of empty ideals.

One of my most respected colleagues died of a brain tumour a couple of years ago. He was a decent and beautiful man who was excellent at what he did but held his achievements lightly. At his funeral we were astounded to learn he was a deeply spiritual man who, in spite of a busy job, would regularly help feed the homeless. This is a life well lived and one we would all do well to aspire to.

The Sacred is an integral part of our work

How do we get a grip on our work life? How do we ensure that every part of our life is informed by all that is good? The answer lies in holding on to all that is sacred in every moment of our lives, including our work lives. Often we forget to invite the Sacred into our work, and so we suffer.

We have no problems in connecting with the Divine when we walk through a forest, or when we are standing alone on a mesa with the wind blowing through our hair. Yet once we leave home in the mornings and make a dash for the train or the plane, already we have forgotten who we are and what sustains us. It is hardly surprising that by the time we are answering emails or packing boxes we seem to be a very different person from the one who sits down to meditate or read a sacred text.

When we lose our connection with the Sacred all the peace and upliftment we have gained from our quiet moments disappears. When we are no longer aware of our divinity or of the divinity that resides in our work mates, the possibilities for positive outcomes fade. Instead of being present in the moment, we find our selves back on the treadmill pedalling as hard and as fast as we can.

We might fool our selves that this is what we have to do to show we have got what it takes, but this is not how to live a full and successful life. We cannot separate our lives into those parts that have sacred moments and those that don't. Our lives are meant to be lived fully, holistically, and so the values and insights and quality of living we attain when in stillness are those aspects that should be present while we work on the assembly line or at the computer.

So accustomed are we to compartmentalising our lives that we don't even realise we are continually cutting our selves off from those things that can help us most. Then when conflict arises, as inevitably it does, we become drawn into the maelstrom. Before we even realise it we are spending huge amounts of our time and energy on politics and backbiting, on rumour and innuendo. Yet again we give in to our clinging mind, to that part of us that loves to enter the fray, to manipulate people and situations, and then we wonder why work seems so unappealing most of the time.

We have all been with friends who are caught up in their work, and have been bored senseless by their endless conversations about their workplace. We are bored by these things, because they are a product of lives that lack purpose and in-sight. When we get involved in all the dramas and intrigues at work, we lose sight of who we are and what we hope to achieve in our job and our lives. Then before we know it all the resulting stress and dissatisfaction from this blinkered way of living spills over into the rest of our lives, contaminating our quiet moments and the time we spend with friends. When we allow our selves to lose sight of our divine magnificence and become embroiled in the minutiae, we only add to our fear and confusion.

When to move forward

When we are able to distance our selves from everything that is happening and see our work life as it really is, we can begin to recognise what needs our involvement and what is best left alone. Navigating our way through the working day with decency and courage and in-sight is one of the greatest challenges we can face on our life's quest. Yet with these challenges comes an invaluable opportunity to discover what is real in our work lives and what is not. This means we have to take a good hard look at all those things that seem attractive, so we aren't seduced by a glittering array of possibilities that work offers, without any awareness of the strings that are attached to these possibilities.

There are times when career success can be even more perilous to our wellbeing than failure. It is easy to end up believing that a company car or a decent pay rise is what life is about. Then, before we realise it, we have vastly inflated views of what work can deliver. How often have we seen decent people sell themselves body and soul for a few more pickings? These things are insidious – they creep up on us in the most unexpected ways.

Losing our selves in our work

Marc had always wanted to open a gallery, but he needed the cash to set up, so he accepted a promotion to help him save the money he needed. Within a couple of years Marc had the funds he required to move on, but then he was offered another promotion and another. A decade later Marc now has enough money to set up several galleries. He still talks about his gallery, except that now he hasn't even the time to get to exhibitions. Marc's whole life has been swallowed up by balance sheets and forecasts. The sad thing is Marc doesn't enjoy what he does, but he no longer has the courage to move on.

Something inside us shrinks when we hear stories like this, because we all want our lives to count for something. But we can only make our passions a reality when there is room in our lives for genuine vision.

Keeping our work in perspective

Certainly we have a right to improve our selves and to honour our achievements, but we must do so lightly, because while these things add to the superficial gloss of life, they can also leave us hungry and desperate for more. Then we find our selves getting drawn into questionable decisions and conduct to satisfy what is required of us.

One dear friend, who had great success in his chosen career, confessed his deep shame at getting to the point where he was obsessing about the size of his office and the location of his car space. This proved to be his wake-up call, because he no longer valued the person he had become. He decided to quit and follow his heart, and now he is a bestselling author whose books sell the world over.

Getting clear about our values

We can't all leave work at the drop of a hat, but we can be clear about the kinds of values we take on at work. We can also recognise those situations that bring out the best in us and those that threaten who we really are, because there are many aspects of work that can bring out our demons.

Often fear gets in the way of our best intentions, causing us to forget who we are and what we are hoping for. This is especially true of those who have worked in organisations where the threat of retrenchment is ever present. In these kinds of demoralising situations, even the most positive people can become intimidated. Motivation and productivity drop away, and everything anyone says or does out of the ordinary is viewed with extreme suspicion.

When we are in these situations, the only way through is to summon the courage to face our fear about whether or not we will have a job next week or next month, and step beyond it. This can be terrifying, yet the more we cling to our fear and to the absolute need of our present job, the more we become paralysed by circumstances.

The universe is here to support us

When we can let go of all the fear surrounding our job and recognise that our welfare is in the hands of the Great Spirit, we can relax into the moment and see where it takes us. This is not about false optimism, but about aligning our selves with the sacred bedrock of life, so we can operate from a solid foundation. When we realise that it is not the managing director or the supervisor or anyone else who is in control of our lives but the all-wise presence of the Great Spirit, we can take back the power we have given away. Then we know we will be at our present workplace as long as we are meant to be there.

We are not always going to be able to prevent the fur flying at work, but we can be in control of our responses to these situations. When we can do this we are able to let go of our attachment to our work, knowing that if we are to move on, another chapter in our lives will unfold for us. This doesn't mean that life won't be challenging, because, like birth, change has its moments. However, the less we are able to hold on to the past or on to the way things might have been, the more effortlessly the future will unfold for us.

When we have the large picture under control, we are less likely to get caught up in the minutiae. We are also able to take things less personally, because we are able to operate beyond the ebb and flow of all the emotions around us. So when clients or work mates are angry, instead of getting defensive, we are more able to listen and to get to the bottom of an issue. Then we discover that we might well have made a mistake, or that behind this anger is a heartfelt plea to help put matters right. Either way we are able to summon our compassion and in-sight to help us deal positively with this situation.

Making the tough calls

This ability to operate outside life's dramas is equally helpful when we have a difficult call to make, because not every decision we arrive at will be a popular or a straightforward one. This need not be an issue as long as the decision we reach is decent and fair. When we live in a space beyond fear, we are less likely to be motivated by the need to play to certain interest groups and more likely be consistent and even-handed. Again this makes us a good person to work with.

Whenever we have to attend a meeting that is likely to be contentious, then not only do we need to prepare all the facts and figures, we need to draw on the strength and in-sight of our sacred centre as well. We can also make the agreed venue a safe place energetically by taking a moment to be still and by asking the Great Spirit to be with us as every part of our being is surrounded with Light. Then, as we contemplate the meeting ahead, we can ask for divine help to arrive at the best outcome for everyone concerned. It helps to visualise the meeting place flooded with Light. Then we can let go of any anxieties, secure in the knowledge that we are protected and guided by the Light.

When we face the person or persons we are meeting with, it also helps to take a moment to silently honour them, to acknowledge that they too are children of the Great Spirit. And as we do so we can consciously bathe everyone present in the Light. If any anxieties arise we simply observe them, then let them pass. Then whatever we say we do so with authenticity and love and simplicity. We don't dwell on the past or on our selves.

As the other person or persons speak, we listen deeply and respectfully to what is being said. We stretch our imagination to allow us to see their perspective and to observe the energy behind their words. When we respond, we acknowledge their feelings with utmost respect. If we feel our selves getting tense, we slow our breathing, then visualise our selves swathed in Light.

As the meeting progresses we hold in our hearts the intention that the issue will be healed in a way that will benefit everyone concerned. Once a resolution is reached, all past thoughts and emotions can now be banished for good as we visualise them being dissolved in Light. As we leave this meeting we can take a moment to thank the Great Spirit and the other person or persons for enabling us to practise our compassion and for all that this situation has taught us.

Always there will be times when we are unable to influence situations, or when there are circumstances that we disagree with. Again this gets back to having the foresight to realise what we can change and what we can't. We are not put here on Earth to involve our selves in everything around us, but to be judicious about where we expend our precious life's energy and why.

Coping with huge workloads

Today one of the many things that gets in the way of our ability to be even-handed is the huge weight of work that most of us deal with. No matter how many lists we write, no matter how much we try to be organised, often we feel as if we are drowning. There is so little time to plan or to get ahead, and no amount of goal-setting seems to help. So yet again we end up chasing our tails.

When we are feeling overwhelmed the only real solution is to step out of the maelstrom and hand the situation over to the Great Spirit, so that we can gain the clarity and in-sight we need to move forward. This is often the last thing we think of doing, yet when we do hand the burden of life back to the Great Spirit, this sacred act not only acknowledges the source of our strength, but aligns us with the laws of the universe as well.

Then we discover just how elastic time really is. Stress causes time to press in on us. Sometimes we can even feel this physically. However, when we step outside a linear concept of time, we enter another relationship with time and space altogether. Here we discover a space that has such an immense sense of expansion and freedom about it that it can feel like a parallel universe. Here we can see things clearly and that we are able to accomplish all we need without effort.

Once we have the courage to step outside the frenzy, our sense of proportion returns and we are able to see the way ahead. Then we will find that the endless piles of work, the terrifying deadlines, the demanding clients are manageable again. I have used this technique many times over, and it really does work. I then find I'll get a call to say a project is delayed or not needed any more, or someone else will offer me their help. Or where there's a complex problem, suddenly the answer will come to me that will not only satisfy all the criteria needed, but more besides.

Once the drama is past, we then need to take a look at how we work. Are we being inefficient or are we saying yes to additional projects when we should say no? Are we overloaded and in need of assistance? Once we know the answers to these questions, we can then address them.

Considering promotion carefully

While the tough times at work challenge us, we also need to be equally clear about our conduct when things are going well. When life is good it is easy to become complacent about our need for the Sacred. The offer of a promotion, for example, may lead us to assume all our problems are solved. We feel loved and appreciated, and a whole new world seems to beckon.

This might well be the case, but it is also easy to be flattered by the possibilities of more money or a bigger brief. We might well be the most suitable person for the vacancy, but it might not be in our best interest to take the position. So we need to ask our selves whether we do actually want the job for its *own* sake.

When we have major decisions to make, we must always remember it is our precious life's energy we hold in the balance. We need to ask our selves whether there is enough benefit in the job to warrant the increased workload and stress, or whether we would prefer to put that additional energy into our own pursuits. On the other hand the promotion might just be what we need to spread our wings and to enhance our creativity and our experience. If so we should accept the new position, remembering that while this promotion might bring much to our lives, it is not our all.

The importance of leadership

If we supervise others, we have additional spiritual responsibilities, because we are in a position to influence the lives of others. One of the greatest threats to our soul progress is when we adopt some of the deeply dehumanising practices and attitudes that are so prevalent in management today. If we profit at the expense of our compassion and decency, if we manipulate people, if we hire and fire without any regard for anything other than the bottom line, we will find our selves on very thin ice karmically, and the wider possibilities for our lives will be severely diminished.

Sometimes the painful effects of our actions might take years to play out, but whatever we sow we reap, and every incidence of the abuse of power and greed and hurt we create will be ours to undo. And so we need always to recognise that we are either creating a path of joy or of sorrow for our selves and others.

Being in charge will stretch us

Leadership is a journey that can be profoundly rewarding, but it can also take us to the depths of despair. People will let us down. They will be ungrateful and thoughtless at times, yet regardless of this, always we must be resolute and even-handed and compassionate. We will need all the foresight and determination we can muster, because no matter how qualified we might be, there will always be a great deal to learn about our selves and others.

When we can open our selves up to our flaws, as well as to new ideas and new ways of seeing and doing things, we are able to benefit from this learning.

If we hope to be a successful leader, we must always stand in a place of truth. We can only do this when we are able to operate beyond fear and beyond all the negative influences we encounter at work. This also means we need to hold a safe space for others, so that those who work with us have the freedom to be honest. They should feel safe enough to tell us when they think we are wrong. When we can allow this level of transparency we enable others to learn the value of truthfulness and authenticity as well. We also make everyone's life easier, because none of us is right all the time.

Creating a culture that works

Part of creating a safe space within and around us is about creating an atmosphere where everyone can be honoured. This means that we need to make time to be there for people. It is easy to get too busy to acknowledge those who work with us, or to do so in such a distracted way that it has no meaning. When, however, we are able to take a genuine interest in those we work with, it warms everyone's lives. There is no better way to exercise our humanity at work than by creating an environment that genuinely recognises the unique contribution of each and every person.

When we do honour those we work with, we create a space where everyone can give of their best, and where each person is able to stand in their own unique space without fear or anxiety. And when each person can honour the other, the whole team becomes strong. Everyone is then able to share in each other's achievements and to support one another when times get tough.

This is a philosophy that most workplaces give lip service to, but one that is rarely borne out in practice. All too often we pit people against each other, and then when one team member wins, everyone else feels resentful. Or because we take no genuine interest in the people we work with, any resulting celebration feels imposed and insincere.

In recent decades working conditions have improved out of hand, but we still have a long way to go. Abuse in the workplace has moved from a physical level to a psychological one, and while exploitation is less obvious, it is still alive and well. Knowing this we need to be clear about our ethics. Good leadership puts the welfare of the team and the organisation before our own.

So focused have we become on the bottom line that many of us have lost sight of how best we can achieve what we need to achieve. When financial results become our all, there is little room for humanity and decency. We encourage some people and discard others, flattering our selves that we are smart operators, until we in turn get pushed out.

Understanding what we can bring to our work

Our working lives can be deeply joyous and fulfilling, but this can only happen when we invite positive values into our working day. Whether we are a leader or not, each and every one of us has something to contribute to our work culture. In times past it was often the canteen ladies or the mail person who cheered our lives, and who were the most remembered, the most loved.

One of the more meaningful ways to change the atmosphere at work is to introduce small rituals to create a more nurturing environment. This is not about living in each other's pockets, but about warming each other's lives with respect and dignity. Often the simplest gestures are the most effective.

I was fortunate to work with a beautiful Chinese woman, who would lighten our lives with fortune cookies and moon cakes and a whole host of things that marked significant moments in the Chinese year. Another work mate used to buy her own funky Post-it Notes for use within the company that again cheered our days.

Healing the workplace

When life is busy it is easy to forget that the work culture is a living entity that is informed by all those who operate within it. If the culture is sick, we have to recognise that we too are part of that malaise. We can help heal this space with our good intentions, our positive energy and even with space clearing.

One practical way to change the energy at work is to visualise the building and all who work in it bathed in Divine White Light. As we do so, we can ask that the Divine Presence allow nothing but goodness and truth to be part of this space, so that there are good outcomes for all who work there. If practised regularly this will help raise the energies in our workplace.

Creating opportunities for joy is always an excellent way to get others over the negativity we often encounter at work. A good friend used to buy her staff Gary Larsen desk calendars just to give them a daily laugh. None of these things is hard, but they can be a lot of fun.

There are times, however, when our workplace isn't just sick it is toxic. When we are in this situation we need to stay true to our sacred practices, so that we can then receive the guidance we need to see the way ahead. If our workplace has become destructive, its work practices questionable, and its climate dark and dangerous, more than likely we need to move on.

If, however, we are meant to stay, we must also realise that no matter how hard it might be to stand up for what is right, life asks that we summon the courage to do so. This does not mean we have to grandstand. Indeed if the atmosphere is difficult, it might not even be appropriate to say anything at all, but simply to remain anchored in our own divinity. When we can remain grounded in our sacred centre, we are a force to be reckoned with, because there is great power in truth and goodness.

One of the greatest gifts that comes with an intimate relationship with the Sacred is the ability to read situations accurately. This isn't just about seeing where the everyday pitfalls lie, but about looking more deeply at our workplace so that we can see where negative energies reside. When we are busy it is easy to ignore the harmful energies around us, but once we are aware of these things we can find ways to protect our selves more effectively from the energies that drain us.

A contemplation on beginning the day positively

Our days flow more easily when we have put aside some time to be alone or to meditate before the busyness sets in. The following visualisation is particularly helpful when we are feeling overwhelmed with our days.

Take a moment to visualise the living sun in all its vivid beauty. Then, as we see the vast ball of swirling yellow before us, we invite it to enter our solar plexus, the centre of our being between our heart and navel. If we can't quite imagine the sun, we can simply imagine its limitless energy and vitality flowing into us. As we absorb the intense yellow of this life-giving force, we imagine it radiating out through every part of us as we are filled with its Light and its Life. We then ask that these energies be anchored deeply and permanently within our being. We can also request that this Light and Life be replenished within us whenever it is needed. It also helps to use this visualisation whenever we feel deep anxiety or distress in the pit of the stomach.

Giving our selves some breathing space

If we hope to maintain our health and vitality once we are at work, we need to extract our selves from the often overwhelming energies we find there, so we can come back to our own sacred centre. This means making an effort to get away from our workspace during the day and, wherever possible, from the building in which we work as well. This might be as simple as finding somewhere to have a sandwich or a cup of coffee, or to have a quick walk around the block.

When we do break for a snack or for lunch, we also need to take great care of the state of mind we are in when we eat, because this is the energy we ingest along with our food. Even if it means having to eat at a less convenient time we should try and avoid stressful or negative conversations around our food. Over the years I have avoided contentious meetings over lunch or dinner for exactly this reason. We don't need to ingest unhelpful energy along with our food. If we are in a situation where we do need to eat, we are far better to resolve the situation, then have a meal. Similarly if there is conflict between workmates, get it solved before eating.

Rarely do we pay attention to our food at work, but it is important, because eating is about nourishing our selves. In the pressure-cooker environment we work in, nurture is often the last thing on our mind. Too often we get busy and skip meals, or we eat at our desks. We get no fresh air and no time to be alone, and then wonder why we feel so out of sorts. Whenever we do go outside we feel more lively, because we have been able to regain our own space. Even a brief trip to the bathroom can make a difference.

Leaving work

When finally we reach the end of the day it is important to switch off from all the pressures so that we can remember who we are beyond the sales targets, the shipping details, or the next order. It helps to free our selves of the day's activity by consciously separating our selves from work, either as we leave our workspace or as we leave the building.

For those who work with computers or machinery it is a good idea to consciously disconnect from them at the end of the day. This can be as simple as saying to oneself, 'My work is done, I am now finished for the day.' It also helps to wash our hands and, if possible, our face, to clear our selves of all the electromagnetic energy we have collected during the day.

Then when we get home it is a good idea to change our clothes. If the day has been particularly stressful, even if our clothes don't need washing it doesn't hurt to wash them or to hang them in the sunshine or the fresh air to remove any negative energy. When we get home it is also important to be conscious of any unhelpful energies we might have brought with us, so that we don't end up contaminating our homes with unhelpful work vibes.

This also goes for discussion about work as well. When things aren't going well it is tempting to deluge those we love with our tales of woe. If we must talk these things over we should be brief, so as not to dampen our precious time together or to foster any negative energies. Again it is better to discuss work matters away from home, and not over meals. An excellent way to review the day is to do so while taking a walk.

Whatever occupation we choose is our decision, and while many work environments have become dark spaces because those who inhabit them have lost their way, work doesn't have to be a penance. We who are Light-bearers can, with the help of the Great Spirit, transform this darkness into the Light of compassion and peace and wisdom. Ours is a task that is greatly blessed and one that holds many wonderful possibilities not only for our selves, but for those with whom we come into contact. So let us use every moment to embrace all that is of the Light. And when our work becomes an integral part of our sacred practice, it will deliver all the passion and in-sight and fulfilment we could hope for.

Contemplations on work

Take a moment now to be still and to go deep within. Then, when you have reached that place of deep calm and profound in-sight, why not consider the following and see what is revealed to you?

- As I stand in my sacred centre I now open myself up to all that my work has to offer me on every level of my being.
- Everything I say and do at work enhances the Light within and around me.
- My working life is filled with endless possibilities to be compassionate and to become wise.
- Everyone with whom I work has the capacity to teach me something about myself and about life.
- As I benefit at work, everyone around me benefits also.
- I give thanks for all that my work brings to my life.

ABOUT SUFFERING

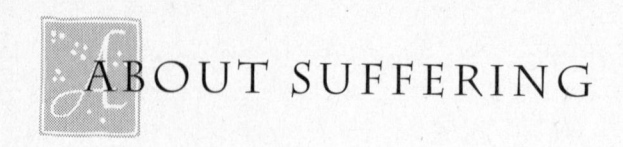

WE CREATE OUR OWN SUFFERING
Most of us are far from amused when times get tough, because we believe that if we work hard and play the game, our life will not only be happy and fulfilled, but without any form of pain or suffering. So strong is our fear of suffering that often we will go to extraordinary lengths to avoid this discomfort.

Then when our partner walks out on us, when we crash the car, or when we have a bitter argument with a close friend, we feel let down. We begin to internalise whatever has taken place, trying to find the reason why this has happened to us. As our demons gather, we play and replay what has taken place, until our world no longer seems a safe place.

When we allow life's disappointments to touch us in this way we become clouded. We cut our selves off from the all-wise inner voice that can show us the way forward. We magnify our suffering as we ignore all the good that already surrounds us. Then we burden our friends and loved ones with our thoughts and feelings, only to end up making everyone more miserable than ever.

Suffering is something most of us feel we can do without, yet all the great spiritual traditions teach us that in amongst life's joys there will be suffering. They also teach that it is our inability to move beyond our need to be constantly happy that prevents us from attaining lasting peace and happiness.

Whether we like it or not, we often have a major hand in those things that upset us. Sometimes we are victims of our own behaviour and sometimes it is our thoughts that lead us astray. Time and again we cling to notions of how life should be, and when things don't work out the way we had intended, we feel let down. So when our only son decides to become a painter instead of a lawyer, or when someone forgets our birthday, or when we don't get the promotion we are in line for, we believe that life has short-changed us.

When we cling to these notions, we fail to consider that our only son might gain all the happiness and fulfilment he could hope for through his painting. Or that by missing out on the promotion, rather than life letting us down, we discover we have missed out on the poisoned chalice that went with the new job as well. When we don't see clearly what is in front of us, we can make serious errors of judgement and end up suffering a great deal.

Siobhan married a man who, while he was kind and attentive, wasn't a wine and roses kind of person. Most of the wonderful things he did went unnoticed, because Siobhan was so caught up in notions of what true love was about. She ended up running off with someone else, who showered her with every gift imaginable. What she didn't realise was that she was funding these extravagances, and when the money ran out, so did the 'love'.

It is not what happens, but how we respond

Whenever we cling to the way we believe things should be, our suffering grows, because we then take everything that happens to us to heart. Convinced that life has it in for us, we become brittle and unforgiving. We even begrudge others what happiness they enjoy.

When we live in a space that is dark and confused, this is the energy we draw to us. And even on the good days whatever joy and kindness might come our way cannot touch us. If we are not careful, we will end up like the tree that is unable to bend in the storm – we will break.

Part of our difficulty in dealing with suffering is that we tend to regard it as failure or as some kind of punishment, when in fact it is just another thread in the rich tapestry of life. Of course we are devastated when things go wrong. And still we have to deal with the shock and the sorrow, but we don't need to allow these things to blight our lives.

The universe will never let us down

No matter how threatened or weary we might be at times, it is no cause for despair, because we have far more going for us than our physical circumstances. Whether we realise this or not, we have all the help we need to see us through. Again when we can harness our understanding of the power and protection of the Light, we can begin to pick our selves up and get on with life.

Someone who is very dear to me almost died recently. I desperately wanted to be with her, but was unable to be. So shocked was I when I got the phone call, I felt numb, and although I prayed desperately that she receive all the healing Light possible, my prayers were confused and driven by fear. Then, after a couple of hours, my inner voice reminded me that my anxiety was of no help.

In an instant the fog of confusion lifted and I was reminded that time and space could not alter the love we shared. I was then able to ask clearly and confidently that whatever healing she required would be hers. At night before I slept I would surround us both in Light, and ask that we might journey to the halls of healing together. This went on for some weeks, then one night my request was refused. Although I had no idea what this meant, I felt strangely calm. The following day her family rang to say all was well, the danger had passed.

Whatever difficulty we are facing is yet another experience in the vast canvas of life. When we can keep things in perspective we are taken beyond our physical bodies, beyond our time on Earth even, to a space that is far more profound. When we use suffering to help us flex our spiritual muscles, we discover the magnitude of the divinity within and around us. It is always there to sustain us and to guide us.

Locating the guidance we need

When we are in a place of deep sorrow, the secret is to be present in the situation no matter how painful, so that we can observe what is happening. Then we can draw on the wisdom and insight we need to see our way through.

The more we connect with the Sacred, the more we are open to the support available to us. This might be as simple as an encouraging smile on a stranger's face or a generous word when we need it most. Whatever assistance we receive, it will be perfect for that moment in time.

Finding the centre of absolute calm

When we are able to hold our suffering more lightly, we learn the courage to pick our selves up and walk into the heart of the difficulty. There, to our surprise, we will find an extraordinary space filled with an all-encompassing calm. This space lies at the centre of all turmoil. When we are able to reach this place, we are able to put all the frenzy and emotions aside and see what is actually going on.

When we learn to head for the eye of the storm, we will be amazed at our capacity to cope. All the remarkable men and women who work in disaster relief understand this concept well. They are able to operate effectively in appalling situations, because they have trained themselves to move beyond the shock and the horror to a place of stillness, so they can help those who desperately need them. It takes strength and courage to rise above our fears, but that is what the adventure of life is about. When we are able to enlist the power of the Light to attain the calm we need, we will then find we are well equipped to do whatever is required of us.

Each situation, no matter how serious, has a centre of calm, and we can use it to help us through any kind of demanding situation. I have used this many times – even at the dentist and while awaiting surgery. It helps immensely, because it gives us the courage to move with and through situations, rather than being paralysed by them. When we can journey through the difficult times in life in this way, not only are our lives easier, so are the lives of those around us as well.

Transforming our suffering into something of worth

The only value in suffering is when we can gather up all the pain and shock and despair and transform it into something worthwhile. Then no matter what happens we are able to stay true to the Light within us, and to discover a depth of in-sight and strength and courage even we didn't know we possessed. Then as we grow through these situations, we do become wise.

There are many wonderful role models around us who work

daily to transmute the suffering and pain of those around them. For years Mother Teresa transformed the despair and pain of the dying on the streets of Calcutta into a space that enabled those unfortunate people to die with dignity and peace. Once we start to grasp the possibilities for our lives we too will be inspired to do what we can.

Discovering the hero within us all

When we are in a particularly painful space, it is easy to withdraw into our selves and assume that this suffering is all about us. However, rarely in any moment of our lives is anything purely about us.

Sometimes life needs us to be in a place of suffering for the benefit of those around us, so that we can light the way for others. When we witness an accident part of us would prefer to run off, but the decent part of us insists we stay and help those in need. It is out of these very situations that extraordinary acts of bravery are born, where ordinary people end up rescuing families from burning buildings or kids from drowning.

While some difficult situations require us to act quickly and decisively, others need us to remain where we are and see the situation through, even though we might be desperate for a way out. When this is asked of us we need to realise such situations are not sent to punish us, but to benefit us in some way. Should we act prematurely we are likely to cause our selves and others more pain.

The universe doesn't ask that we take everything that comes to us without resistance, but that we have sufficient faith to hold a steady course. So when we continue to get out of bed in the morning and feed the family regardless of what is happening, we participate in another kind of heroism that stretches us beyond our own needs, enabling us to help those who are dependent on our goodwill and decency.

This is the heroism we see in mothers the world over, who struggle to feed and care for their families in countries ravaged by war or by famine. When we too can face all that comes our way with equanimity, we are able to discover our own inner heroism. The stronger we are, the stronger we enable those around us to be.

Understanding life's quest

Often we suffer because we don't fully understand the nature of life on Earth. We arrive here and settle in, surrounding our selves with what comforts we can, and then we go into spiritual hibernation. We forget that all things on the Earth plane are temporary. Then when our children leave home, or when we lose our relationship or our job, we are devastated. The impermanent nature of earthly life wasn't constructed to hurt us, but to point us forward so that we can build our lives on things that have permanence, that will advance our soul's journey.

At some level we know this already. The secret is to live consciously with this understanding, then we are able to fully enjoy all that our children, our partner or our career can bring us. When the time comes to say goodbye, instead of drowning in our sorrow or despair, we can genuinely help those around us by blessing them as they move on, bathed in the Light of our goodwill.

Things aren't always going to go our way

Suffering comes to us to help make us even more magnificent than we already are, and to propel us into a new space. When we understand there are always going to be moments of disappointment, moments when we miss out on a pay rise or when the man or woman of our dreams has other plans, rather than trying to reopen the door that has slammed resoundingly in our faces, we need to gather up our life's energy in readiness for the right moment to move on, recognising that when one door shuts more often than not a whole lot of windows fly open.

Suffering can be most overwhelming when it catches us unawares. Then it is easy to feel betrayed. Our natural impulse is to try and get our lives back in control. Yet it is not control that we need at these times, so much as the ability to see clearly where this painful circumstance is leading us. When we suddenly find our selves seriously ill or retrenched or bereaved, we are at our most vulnerable, and because we are forced to rely on those around us, often we feel at the very edge of our endurance. Again we can choose to expend our life's energy on all the negative thoughts and emotions that assail us, or we can embrace what is happening to us and move forward to reach the centre of calm within this situation.

When we are in a difficult place, it is tempting to give in to our terror, because life can seem frightening all of a sudden. We need instead to realise that in spite of how things might seem, we are not at the edge of an abyss. Rather we are in the place of all possibilities, which may well transform our lives.

When we can project our selves beyond all the pain and misery of a particular moment, life's magic and grace will reveal itself to us. This book was born in such a moment. It was while I was unable to walk that I realised it was time to share the many blessings life had brought me. Often it is only after we have had a break-up or a brush with a fatal illness that we have the strength and vision to be where we want to be, doing the things we love. When we can see this, even misfortune becomes our friend.

Assisting those who suffer

One of the more challenging aspects of dealing with suffering is helping those around us who suffer. We can't live their lives for them, but we can hold on to a good outcome to help see them through. When we do try to assist others we have to take special care not to get drawn into their pain. Instead we must seek to raise their energy by our own encouraging words, and by holding fast to the Light, so that we can hold a sacred space for them.

It is important we continue to meditate, so we can deepen our understanding of what is going on for them. As we anchor ourselves in this energy, we can call on the Great Spirit to be with us. As we settle into meditation, we can then ask to journey to the centre of our loved one's painful situation. As we journey deep within, we will see our beloved in their suffering, and then beyond it. And as we hold on to this latter image, we realise that first and foremost they too are fellow spiritual beings on their own extraordinary journey through life.

We can then ask that the universal healing energy will be theirs on whatever levels of their being is most appropriate. This might mean they are healed of a physical or mental affliction, or it might mean that healing has been activated purely at a soul level. The important thing is we are simply the conduit for this healing energy, and that through this opportunity we are able to give them the best support possible.

When we take part in such healing opportunities, always we must do so with humility, because we have no idea of the full scope of this person's soul journey. Even if they are terminal, healing can still take place. While they might not be cured of their illness, through our prayers and through the Light we hold in our hearts, we can help illuminate their passage.

About Suffering

Absent healing

If we are not able to be with our loved one in person, still we can bless them with this meditation, because there are no boundaries to the healing power of the universe. And whenever our loved one comes to mind, we can continue to surround them with Love and Light. Even though we might not appreciate the full value of such acts, we can rest assured that all the warmth and genuine caring that this energy brings will profoundly touch the life of our loved one wherever it is needed most.

Beyond suffering

As we walk the path of the Sacred we learn to move beyond suffering, not because life ceases to be painful, but because no longer do those things have any hold over us. As we each gain more Light in our lives, eventually we move beyond our desires and fears to a space of pure being that is untouched by whatever suffering comes our way. When we meet high souls their all-encompassing wisdom and calm is more than apparent. So awesome is their Light that it literally takes the breath away. While we might not have arrived at this place yet, the important thing is that we are heading in the right direction.

The truly successful life is the life well lived, where all the disappointments, all the losses and grief can be seen as sacred opportunities, and where like the alchemists of old we are able to gather up the base matter of our lives and transform it into gold.

Contemplations for times of suffering

Find a place that is quiet where you love to be, and as you enter the Silence take time to reflect on some or all of the following:

- I now embrace the difficulty I face, knowing that I can benefit from this situation.

Coming Home

- I am present in this moment of suffering, so that I may benefit from all the in-sight and guidance and wisdom this situation can bring.
- I welcome this opportunity, however challenging, to continue to enhance the Light within my own being.
- No matter what happens in life, I am never, ever alone.
- I open myself up to all the learning that comes to me in this moment.
- I always inhabit a space that is safe and supportive.

How do we love the unlovable?

*Those who wrong me, and those who accuse me
falsely, and those who mock me, and others:
may they all be sharers in Enlightenment.*
SANTIDEVA, 'Entering the Path of Enlightenment'

OUR NEEDS CAN MAKE US VULNERABLE

How do we deal with those who are hard to love? Do we try to convince our selves that we like them? Do we pretend they don't exist? Do we seek affirmations that will magically transform them? Do we pray that they will go and live on the other side of the world and be out of our lives entirely? Or do we look deep within, discover our own vulnerabilities and gain the in-sight to treat the unlovable with compassion?

Sometimes when we look around we are filled with frustration, because life can be extremely trying at times. As we watch the news and witness acts of unspeakable greed, selfishness and inhumanity, we feel bewildered. Even on good days it is easy to allow others to fracture our happiness and leave us thinking thoughts we would rather not have, let alone give voice to. Learning to deal with those we would rather live without is one of life's more interesting challenges, yet it is also one that, when mastered, can transform our whole experience of life.

When we encounter those we find hard to love, we need to recognise that what affects us most about these people is not so much what is wrong with them as their uncanny ability to strike at the heart of our own woundedness, to expose those parts of us that are in desperate need of healing. Before we can move beyond our active dislike of those we find hard to deal with, we must understand how our own needs make us vulnerable.

When we meet the world from a position of needing to be loved and recognised, we make our selves vulnerable to all the nuances in life that we encounter every day. When we operate from a position of need in life, the world – our world – is not a safe place.

When we are needy we search for recognition wherever we can find it, only to discover that no one seems to be totally on our side. Daily life can seem like one long battle, and the harder our life gets, the further we withdraw into our selves. The unfortunate remark or the ill-timed gesture serves only to highlight our fears and insecurities about our ability to be loved, to be given the recognition we crave. Every time someone touches our woundedness, wittingly or otherwise, we react, and the ache deep inside us grows, until we are left feeling even less hopeful of getting what we need from life.

Taking it personally makes it hurt

It is all too easy to take the universe personally, yet often the person who offends us isn't intending to do so. They might just be naturally blunt, or they might be dealing with a serious problem in their personal lives. When we are bound up in our selves – in who we are and how others should behave towards us – we are blind to the reality of the situation. As a result, when someone seems abrupt or uninterested, or just plain rude, we cannot help but take offence.

How expectations influence outcomes

Often we cling to notions of how we need the world to be, only to discover that other people don't easily fit into the boxes in which we want to place them. Those who love us most often hurt us deeply, while those we don't expect a great deal from can surprise us with their kindness and generosity. This makes life confusing, and we respond by raising our defences. Then when someone says or does something unfortunate we slip into a flight or fight response. Because we are fearful, we automatically assume we are being attacked, and so we cannot help but run away or fight back. All we are doing, however, is magnifying the unhelpful energies in our lives and wasting more time and effort on dealing with the fallout.

Healing our selves

Instead of responding in the heat of the moment, we need to find some quiet time to examine the situation that troubles us and consider how best we might deal with those who provoke us. In the process, we must recognise that the very fact that we are reacting negatively indicates that there is some part of us that is as yet unhealed. Once we discover what needs healing, we will be able to seek help to mend this part of us, to make us whole. We might achieve this by intensifying our spiritual practices, by taking more time to be alone in order to gain further in-sight and space, or by seeking the help of a professional.

Part of the healing process involves establishing a firm foundation to our lives that will give us all the love, all the kudos, all the encouragement, all the strength, all the courage we need to operate in the world. When our lives have this level of vision and sustenance, we no longer need to worry about whether someone respects or acknowledges us, or whether they love us or simply like us a lot. This does not mean we are arrogant. Rather, it means that our lives are anchored in a place of great calm and fulfilment.

This is the experience of living with clarity and depth. It is the extraordinary peace we enjoy when we are finally on our journey home to our true selves. When goodness is our motivation, we can be sure that we are walking the path of Light. When we step beyond those things that limit our experience of our selves and of life, we start to realise just how empowering life can be. And as we hold this understanding in our hearts, we realise the capacity we have to live fully and expansively in a way that benefits all concerned.

In-sight begets compassion

Once we have healed our selves, we are able to turn our attention back to the person who troubles us and recognise their woundedness. As we find time to be still, we are able to see beyond our immediate reactions, beyond our emotions and preconceptions, and glimpse at the heart of the person we have issues with.

As our hearts then open with compassion, our differences start to drop away. We are then able to see this person as they are, not as we assumed them to be. We are able to see behind the abrasive words – the seeming confidence – to their pain, their uncertainty. We see that whatever this person creates in their life is only a reflection of a far greater hurt they carry inside. We see also that the pain they cause others when they are unforgiving or selfish, when they are mischievous or manipulative, is their way of dealing with their suffering.

This does not mean that we allow people to be cruel or abusive. We must always be clear about what is acceptable and what is not. When, however, our lives are inspired by the Sacred, we are able to respond differently to those who are hard to love. As our hearts open with compassion for this person, we see what they need most in their lives is not to have yet another person avoid them or disapprove of them, but to have a little more kindness, a little more understanding. We can see that they need people they can trust, people whom they can feel genuinely safe with, so that they, in turn, might be a little less fearful. We also realise that the volatile work mate doesn't get out of bed in the morning with the intention of making us miserable, but that they are unpredictable because they live in fear of life spinning out of control.

As our in-sight increases, so does our compassion, until we are able to deal with this person lightly and without any expectation, aware that our life's quest is not to try to take charge of their life but simply to shine our Light of compassion and hope where we can. This might mean being more assertive in our dealings with this person, or it might mean staying out of their way altogether. Instead of getting angry or criticising them, always we must be positive, praying that they might also achieve their highest good. We must bless them and ask that they be released from those aspects of life that bind them, so that they too may journey home.

BEING IN-SIGHTFUL RATHER THAN JUDGEMENTAL

It is not up to us to judge another person or speculate about them with others. We are not the Great Spirit. We must also remember that no matter how desperate the situation, nothing in the universe is impossible. Even those who appear beyond hope can surprise us: Milarepa, Tibet's greatest saint, was a black magician and a murderer, yet after a great deal of intensive spiritual work his life was utterly transformed.

There are times when the person we face seems so formidable that we doubt our ability to change things in any way. Sometimes we can be so intimidated by such people that we go to the lengths of leaving our job or relationship to avoid them, only to discover the same problems awaiting us further down the track. Unless we are in an abusive situation – in which case we must leave – we need to look again at our selves and attempt to understand why we are feeling overwhelmed or fearful.

Years ago I had a talented work mate who had a blatant disregard for women. No matter what anyone said or did, it was impossible to alter his attitude. One day I learned that the woman he had devoted his life to had run off, leaving him with massive debts. As soon as I knew this, everything became clear. When I recalled his many outbursts I could also see his terrible hurt and was deeply moved by it. I had no idea I could care so much about a person who had made my life and the lives of many others so hard. Yet once I became more understanding and, consequently, more compassionate, he became gentler and more trusting.

We never spoke about what had happened – we didn't need to. What mattered was that my change in attitude had made his shattered world a little safer, and whenever he had a meltdown, I no longer took it personally. And because I didn't react, over time his behaviour improved greatly.

Most of us want our lives to be positive, to count for something. But sometimes it is hard to hold this vision when we see how much more decency and compassion is needed in life. We keep on hoping that someone will do something dramatic – something that will make a big difference – forgetting our own immense capacity for goodness, forgetting that daily we have the opportunity to shine what Light we possess into the dark places in life.

How Do We Love the Unlovable?

Letting our Light shine

When times are challenging, we must be mindful of how we conduct our selves. No matter how tempting it might be to retaliate, to harm the other party by word or deed, we must not do so. No matter how weary or hurt or despairing we might be, we must never add to the darkness in life. Instead, we need to pray for the wisdom and compassion and inspiration to deal with the situation before us in the best way possible.

We need also to ask to be shown the lesson to be learnt from this experience, in the knowledge that once we have worked on it, no longer will it be an issue in our lives. Then we will be able to appreciate that even the most difficult people can be part of our journey towards wholeness.

We *can* make a difference

As we stretch our capacity to love beyond those who are easy to love, we begin to understand what an awesome thing it is to genuinely love another. We begin to see and experience for our selves the immense healing that comes as we transmute pain into joy, despair into hopefulness. We realise that love is not just another concept, but a force that is real and available to us without condition or expectation.

Then we feel free to embrace goodness for goodness' sake, knowing that every time we send out Love and Light to those around us it will touch someone's life where it is needed most. And whatever we send out will be returned to us many times over.

One of the great and irrefutable laws of life is that love is a powerful healer: when it is given freely, its gentleness has far more ability to effect change than the endless avalanche of words and actions that are so prevalent in our lives.

Each of us holds within us more power than we could dream of. By our actions we influence the advancement or otherwise of all sentient beings. And when we summon the courage to advance the Light, we not only contribute to the betterment of humankind, we also actively lessen all that is dark and painful.

There is much in contemporary life to disempower us, to make us feel less than we truly are, but how we react to these things is up to us. We hold the key to our success. All we need is the courage to make it our own. In good times and bad, we can make a serious difference on this tiny planet of ours.

A prayer to help us deal with those we find hard to love

'O, Great Spirit, teach me courage and strength so that always I enhance the Light in the world. Help me never to judge those around me. Help me to learn to see deeply into the hearts of all I meet, so that I can discover what it is within others that links us all, that makes us all one. And may all that I think and say and do be informed by compassion and goodness and truth, so that the space I occupy is safe for myself and for all I meet.'

UNDERSTANDING OUR EMOTIONS

LEARNING TO LIVE WITH OUR EMOTIONS

So here we are on Earth, spiritual beings exploring all that it means to be human. Ours is a remarkable quest and a demanding one also. There are so many dimensions to our earthly adventure that it is easy to become lost in the detail, to lose sight of who we are and what we are here to achieve. And as with most quests often we don't fully understand how to use the tools we have been given, so we are unable to benefit from them.

This is true of our emotions also. At best our emotions can enhance every aspect of our daily lives. They can bring us light and shade, love and friendship and nurture, and much more besides. They can also destroy us and those we love.

We don't want to live without our emotions. We just want to find a way to live with them that works. We can only do this when we fully understand the valuable role our emotions can play in our lives, and when we realise the impact they have on every level of our being.

When we take care of our emotions we take care of our selves – mind, body and spirit. We need to get a grip on our emotional selves, because while we seem resilient, we are in fact incredibly intricate as beings, and when our emotions are out of control they have an immediate impact on us.

When life is going well, when we are healthy and happy, we benefit physically, mentally and spiritually. When we are stressed and unhappy our wellbeing is eroded and every part of us is affected. We are also affected by what is going on in the outside world, and so we must take particular care as to what we allow into our lives.

Treating our life energy with care

Every day we use a great deal of energy. Even the effort required to get through an average day can be considerable. Yet because we already enjoy a certain level of vitality, it is easy to take this for granted, until we get sick, then we understand how devastating life can be when our energy has deserted us. What few of us realise is that our emotions draw from our life force as well, and so we need to be very clear about which emotions we give our energy to and why.

Much has been written about the effects of diet and sleep and exercise on our wellbeing, but only now are we becoming aware of the far-reaching effects that unchecked emotions can have on the health of our minds and bodies and spirits.

The impact of our emotions at a soul level

We are extremely vulnerable to our emotions at a soul level. This level of our being is made up of countless delicate threads of light that encompass every part of us, and because these threads are impossibly fine they are easily damaged. In balanced lives these threads form a perfect pattern that is able to absorb the highest spiritual energies we are capable of receiving. These energies then enliven and uplift us as they move through every part of our being. When our soul threads are undisturbed we are in perfect balance, and we feel at one with our selves and the world.

Understanding Our Emotions

If our emotions are allowed to rage through our bodies, not only do we feel the effects of these destructive energies on our minds and bodies, but at a soul level also. So when we become upset or depressed or resentful, our soul threads become hopelessly tangled and torn, and our capacity to receive the higher spiritual energies is greatly diminished.

When we allow our emotions to flare, we sabotage all the progress we have made at a soul level. We often complain that while we are working hard to lead decent lives we feel as if we are making no progress, and we are right. When we are not masters of our emotions, all the positive work we have put in to raise our vibrations is constantly eroded.

When we allow negative emotions to be part of our lives and take up residence within us, sooner or later they become toxic and have a very real impact on our physical health. And long before the resulting health problems are apparent, these destructive energies spill over into our work lives and into our homes and friendships, poisoning all that is good there.

Taking charge of our emotions

The choice of how we expend our precious life's force is ours to make every moment of every day. We need only visit a friend who is seriously ill or dying to be reminded just how precious our life force is. We can start to get our emotions under control by observing the people and situations that spark these unfortunate responses within us.

Once we can recognise these flash points, we can be clearer about how we handle our selves. Then we have good reason to pause before we get involved with the difficult neighbour or the demanding relative. Instead we can ask our selves whether we are going to waste our time and life energy on this, or whether we have got something better to do with our day. Even when we do let our emotions get the best of us, at least then we will be more conscious about what we have done, and will be a little more reluctant to do so again.

When our soul threads are first revealed to us it is an awesome moment. So exquisite is their intricate pattern, so impossibly delicate the fabric of Light that moves through them, that we can hardly believe what we are seeing. Once we know about our soul threads we are then able to discover what is happening within us at any time. We also begin to realise the damage we do to ourselves when we allow our emotions to get the better of us.

It is not only negative emotions that cause us damage

All emotions that are excessive harm us. And so we need to take care not to become overly excitable, because this too makes demands on our life force and on our soul threads. We all know how exhausting it can be when we are around those who are hyperactive or happy, happy, happy. We feel worn out, because we are being drained by this energy. This is why in spiritual practice such importance is placed on moderation, because immoderate behaviour can and does harm us.

Extreme exhaustion also affects us as well. It causes our soul threads to lose shape and hinders the passage of Light through our bodies. When we are upset or angry the damage to our system is even more pronounced. We will actually see dramatic tears in our soul threads.

Waking up to the emotions around us

It is not just *our* emotions we need to be conscious of, but the emotions of all those around us – at home and at work, in our families and friendships. Often the emotions that harm us most are the unchecked emotions of the people we deal with – of those who can't keep their tempers under control, those who are in a perpetual state of upset or despair, or those who are continually anxious or resentful.

Often these unacceptable patterns of behaviour have become so much part of our life that we are not even aware of them. These negative energies are then absorbed into our being as well. When we spend time with a friend or family member who drains us, when we listen yet again to all the tales of self-pity or woe they regale us with, when we go to work and deal with work mates who are moody, who can't keep their emotions under control, basically we are under siege, and then we wonder why our life is so stressful and frustrating so much of the time.

A VISUALISATION FOR VULNERABLE MOMENTS

When we are feeling fragile and in need of support it helps to go deep within and to visualise a disc of rose pink being absorbed into our hearts, and to feel it warming our being, and radiating out from here into our lives and reassuring us that all will be well. As we invite this healing energy in, we can then ask that it be anchored deep within us. This simple exercise helps with feelings of extreme vulnerability. And should these feelings return, instead of becoming lost in our fears, we can simply visualise this rose-pink disc surrounding our heart and stilling our anxieties.

BEING MINDFUL OF OUR CONDUCT

As we seek to gain mastery over our emotions, we need also to be aware of the emotionally draining situations we deal with daily. This applies as much to our conduct as to the conduct of those around us. We then begin to recognise all the times we burden others with our complaints and our gossip and speculation. These too are emotionally laden habits that are destructive for all concerned. Once we are able to recognise this for our selves, then when we do forget our selves and get involved in rumour and innuendo, we will discover just how drained and joyless we feel.

Emotions are energies

Emotions in themselves are neither good nor bad. It is the way we use our emotions that is critical. When we misuse our emotions we are coming from a place of lack – of needing to be noticed, or to be acknowledged. When we are reliant on the outside world and feel unable to get what we want, our negative emotions will start to overtake us. And if we are not careful, in our hurt or disappointment we will then feed these emotions, and before we know it they are out of control.

An important part of mastering our emotions is about placing our lives on a firm foundation. When we come from a place of lack we are vulnerable to the ebb and flow of circumstances around us. Often we will go to extraordinary lengths to keep our selves buoyant, yet this kind of superficial happiness does not help, because it is just another mask for our desperation, our despair.

Many of us in the West have come to believe that unless we are experiencing some kind of extreme emotion we are not really alive. Sadly this is the very kind of thinking that leads people to problems with drugs and alcohol, and compulsions of every kind. There are many exhilarating and awesome ways to feel truly alive in this extraordinary universe of ours, and the path of the Sacred, not our emotions, will deliver on this.

Life beyond our emotions

It is only when we progress beyond the demands of our emotions that we enter a deeper reality, where even the everyday aspects of life have an exquisite feel to them. The ancients described this space as the golden mean and the Buddhists as the middle way. This way of living enables us to move beyond the highs and lows, so that we can inhabit a place that is untouched by neediness of any kind.

This place of indescribable peace and deep joy exists beyond the angst and the desperation that characterises so much of our waking lives. When we reach this space, instead of expending all our energy on trying to stay happy, we are able to move purposefully and insightfully through the day, savouring each moment as it unfolds.

There is no room for boredom or blandness in this sacred place, because it enables us to experience life deeply, profoundly. It is a space of great ease, where no part of our precious life's energy is ever wasted. It is a state that demands less action and more awareness, and where each day, each hour, each moment is an experience to be savoured.

Healing our woundedness

Different emotions affect each of us. For some it is anger we wrestle with, and for some it is doubt or fear, while for others it is all of these things. One of the areas we ignore is our capacity to worry. This too erodes our wellbeing and draws from our life force. We have a responsibility to deal with our worry, not only because these negative energies drag us down, but because they do the same for those we are worrying about. In a very real way when we worry we are burdening the lives of those we love with the inappropriate use of our emotions. Instead we are better to ask that the situation that is worrying us be filled with Light, then ask for the guidance we need to see if anything further should be done.

Once we recognise our emotional patterns we can do something about them. Then, when our emotions threaten to overwhelm us, instead of getting caught up in the tensions of the moment we learn to become still. As the emotional storm passes, we can look deeply and without judgement at that part of us that sparks these emotions, and discover what is lacking there.

Once we see this we can ask that this dark place within be filled with healing Light and Love. As we work with the Light and our knowledge of our soul threads, we can free our selves from the emotions that created this woundedness. We do this by holding on to all that is sacred in our lives, and by refusing to nurture negative emotions. When unwanted emotions arise, we are then able to anchor our selves in our sacred centre, observe the unhelpful emotions and let them pass. Every time they return, we simply observe them and let them go. If we have more serious emotional problems, of course we are wise to seek the help of a practitioner, and preferably one who can treat our whole being.

Some days we will be pleased with the way we have kept our emotions in check, and other days we will feel we have failed altogether. Always we must be gentle on our selves. We need to know our willingness to pick our selves up when we haven't succeeded as well as we had hoped is a vital part of our life's quest.

At the same time we must remember that life is an adventure that should be exhilarating and expansive and fun. When we can approach our emotions in this way, we will be able to progress more quickly, knowing that every step we take is a step closer to freeing our selves of the emotions we don't need.

The more we progress the easier it is for us to deal with our emotions, not just because we are more conscious of any likely conflict within or around us, but because we start to inhabit a more peaceful space. Then every time we venture beyond it we are able to pull our selves back, because it becomes increasingly unpleasant to experience disharmony of any kind.

USING OUR EMOTIONS AS THEY WERE INTENDED

While our emotions need to be handled with care, they aren't all bad. When used positively we are able to use them to explore the awesome nature of all that it means to be human. We can then use our ability to feel pain and despair to enable us to be more loving to those who need our love. After all, if we had never known what it feels like to be sad or hurt or lonely, how could we ever express our loving-kindness to those in need? When we can harness our feeling self to love our selves and to help others, and to experience the beauty and complexity and deep mystery of earthly life, we are using our emotions as they were intended.

When we can transmute our anger and resentment into positive energies to help save forests and rivers, to feed the hungry and to speak out against man's inhumanity to man, then again we can use our emotions for immense good. Even our fear can be worthwhile, when it gives us the presence of mind to protect our selves and others in moments of danger. And so as we heal our selves we heal others, not by spectacular works or deeds, but by simply who we are.

A meditation to help us work with our soul threads

Find a place to sit or lie down where you can be quiet and comfortable. Then, as you gently close your eyes, bring your attention back into your body. As you breathe in and out, allow every part of you to become heavy. If there are any areas of your body that feel tense, continue to breathe slowly as you allow them to relax. Now and always you are in the presence of the Great Spirit. Knowing this, take a moment to savour this the most sacred of Presences. Feel the boundless love and wisdom surrounding and supporting you.

Then, as you continue to follow your breath, bring your attention deep into your body. Allow yourself to focus on your body and give thanks for this magnificent earthly home to your spirit. Give thanks for your life and for all that it has brought you, for all you have experienced and learned, for all the sustenance and nurture that is yours. What an extraordinary journey is human life!

And now, as your attention rests in your body, you are reminded of all the times you have forgotten or neglected this remarkable body of yours. In a desire now to love and cherish this awesome vehicle of flesh and blood, ask to see your soul threads. Hold no preconceptions of how they might reveal themselves to you. If you are not a visual person, then simply ask that you be given a word or an image that best describes the state of your soul threads. Then, as they present themselves, allow yourself a moment to contemplate the intricacy of the life that is yours. If your soul threads are stretched out before you in all their perfection, enjoy this moment as you observe the many tiny rivulets of Light that nourish every part of your being.

If your soul threads seem limp they are showing you how weary you are right now. Accept this and ask for the Great Spirit's Healing Light to bring them back to their perfection. Watch the miracle of your soul threads becoming strong once more, and feel the immediate difference throughout

Understanding Our Emotions

your whole being. Feel the life and the Light filling you utterly, as you give thanks for this moment of wholeness.

If your soul threads are torn or damaged in some way, simply accept this and ask the Great Spirit to restore them. And again, as you see the many strands of your soul threads returning to their perfection, how much better you feel as this healing transforms and illuminates your being, as your heart opens with gratitude to receive such bounty.

Take a moment or two to rest in this perfection. Know that you are now receiving the highest spiritual vibrations you are capable of. How beneficial this is for you. Experience what it is like to be whole. Feel the immense joy and peace. This is your natural state and the one in which you are most able to thrive. Recognise it and honour it. This is your birthright. This is yours to enjoy each and every moment of your lives. Take a moment now to give thanks for this experience:

'O, Great Spirit, thank you for my life and for all the many layers of my being that enable me to live fully and joyously on this earthly plane. I now ask that Your Divine Presence inform each and every day of my life. Help me to master my emotions, so that I might use them for the greatest good today and always.'

And now, as you hold the energy of Divine Light and Goodness in your heart, may It illuminate all those places that are dark and difficult, so that each day you may walk in the Light.

THE VALUE OF RITUAL

THE STEPPING STONES TO THE DIVINE
Often our lives are so busy that the weeks and months slip past, and before we know it another year has gone. Yet when we look back and try to remember what we have done with the year, it is often hard to pinpoint anything much that is worthwhile beyond the daily routine of home and work.

When, however, we take time to look a little more deeply at our lives, we begin to see that the Divine is with us wherever we are. We start to realise that even when we are dashing to and from work, when we are picking up the groceries or taking the dog for a walk, there the Divine waits for us – waits for that moment, when we will step beyond our busyness and take notice of the many riches that lie beyond all this activity.

TRANSFORMING THE ORDINARY INTO THE EXTRAORDINARY
When we allow our selves the freedom to look beyond the familiar, we discover the many opportunities that are there for us to transform even the most mundane aspects of our lives into something that has more depth, more joy, more purpose.

One of the ways we can tap into the deep joy of life is through

The Value of Ritual

ritual, through consciously inviting the Sacred into every aspect of our lives. Rituals were once an integral part of everyday life. Today most of our rituals are so commercial as to be almost meaningless.

Yet if our lives can't be joyous, memorable and interesting, why bother getting out of bed in the morning? Without a sense of life's magic and fulfilment in our everyday lives we are little more than sleepwalkers drifting through life with nothing to look forward to, and nothing to distinguish one day from the next.

When approached with sacred intent, rituals can inject our everyday lives with a far greater sense of meaning. They are well able to connect us with that which lies within and beyond us, and can help us escape our own inertia to inject a greater sense of joy and purpose into our everyday lives.

Rituals are as old as humankind

For thousands of years rituals have been one of the means by which we have celebrated our lives and the lives of those around us. They have also been an important means by which we can reflect on our place within the universe. We all need time to reflect and to celebrate our life's journey, and rituals can still be an invaluable way of doing this. As long as we realise that their only value is in their ability to reflect a far greater truth, they will enrich our quest.

Even though we must attend to our many commitments, our lives need not be lacklustre. When we invite the occasional ritual into our lives, we give shape and form to the immense beauty and privilege of life – we nudge our selves beyond the daily routine, giving our lives markers that help us distinguish one week from the next. As long as we never come to rely on these rituals, they will bless our lives greatly.

One of my most treasured memories of my early years is of Sunday mornings with my father. Rain, hail or shine he would take my sister and me to the woods, to that magical realm where he would bring each precious moment to life by pointing out all the things we hadn't noticed. While his job was physically demanding and there were no doubt times when he would rather have stayed in bed, he would take us off to while away a few hours ankle deep in leaves or in bluebells, or watching dragonflies hover over the streams.

Then when I was a little older my mother would take my sister and me into the city during school holidays. There we would shop, and have sandwiches and cake at an old-world cafe. Even now the memory of these days thrill me. Mine was not a privileged childhood, but it was rich in experiences that warmed the heart and fed the soul. And through these and many other opportunities I was able to begin to appreciate the many textures of life.

Opportunities for mindfulness

When used as they were intended, rituals are about being alive to what is going on in and around us. At best they are simple and laden with meaning. They enable us to experience the deep joy of being and of capturing a particular moment in time. Some rituals enable us to celebrate the importance of those we love, while some enable us to enjoy a rare chance to be alone. How each ritual is constructed is of less importance than this magnificent opportunity to be present enough to take joy in the moment, to explore its every aspect and to hold it in our hearts.

All too often we allow these opportunities to slip through our fingers, because our attention is elsewhere. We miss out on all the joy and the immense sense of release that these moments can bring. Then not only does one day slip into the next, but so too do whole segments of our lives, until we end up missing out on all the exquisite nuances and the inherent wisdom that each new chapter of life brings us.

If we lived in more traditional societies, for example, we could not fail to notice the change of seasons, let alone celebrate them. Those who live closer to the earth understand well the rhythm of life. For them the celebration of the seasons is a celebration of life and food and all the possibilities that come with each new cycle of the year. They honour the cycle of life and in honouring it they are able to benefit from all the bounty it brings.

We can still seize the moment and embrace the seasonal magic that is all around us. We can still walk in the park and revel in the spring flowers planted there. We can enjoy summer picnics and watch the leaves turn to rust and gold. We can still make an effort to walk in the snow and the mist and the rain. These are all sacred moments awaiting us, moments that can warm our lives now and for years to come.

Rituals present us with wonderful ways not only to appreciate the texture and substance of our lives, but to reach out to those around us. So as we spend time with family and friends we are able to be kind, to give something of our selves and to allow others to do the same. There are many rituals available to us that we can share with others, that can inject a renewed sense of meaning into all our lives.

Rediscovering the depth in the rituals we already have

Although many of the rituals available to us have become lost in commercialism, still we can go deeper and discover the profound wisdom and in-sight that is concealed there. Easter is a beautiful time to get together with those we love. It is also the perfect time to contemplate the life of the Master Jesus – to meditate on the awesome nature of the Christ and all that His Divine Energy can bring to our lives.

Similarly when we consider Valentine's Day, we have the opportunity to transform this celebration of romantic love into something much more profound and satisfying. How special this day would be if we were to use it to honour all those we love, and all those whose love sustains us. With Mother's Day we have the opportunity not only to honour our mothers, but to honour the Great Mother Earth – to celebrate her bounty and her awesome beauty. What an exquisite possibility we have to combine the two in some way.

What we are seeking in these experiences is the chance to live with more joy, to celebrate what it means to be alive, and to embrace the best of all that is around us. When we do so we make each moment, each interaction, a sacred one. Again we can only do this when we live mindfully, when we are aware of where our life's energy is going.

Too often our creativity is expended on our commitments at home and at work. Yet if we were to apply even a fraction of this effort and imagination to the shape and substance of our lives, they would be transformed. None of us has as much time as we would like but we can all be more creative about how we use it.

Simplicity and authenticity are the keys to rituals that serve us well

In seeking to give our lives greater depth and texture, we are not trying to make our lives busier but looking for opportunities to add to the experience of life. Often when we think of doing something new or different, we fail to keep things simple so we are unable to enjoy what we are doing, let alone sustain it.

After a number of happy years of sharing a house, several friends went their separate ways. They still lived in the same city and were keen to keep in touch. They decided to meet at a cafe once a week. While not everyone was able to turn up each week, there were always enough people to sustain this happy gathering, and because of this the strong friendships that had developed over the years remained.

This kind of get-together is reminiscent of the years when extended families would congregate for Sunday lunch or dinner. Most of us don't have the time and energy for a weekly get-together, but we can still gather together now and again to share in the warmth of human kindness and company.

Injecting more light and shade into our work lives

When we consider the possibilities for ritual we mustn't forget about our work lives. It is always uplifting to keep thankyou notes and inspirational cards. My office is littered with angel cards, because they help me to sustain the energy I need to maintain and enhance my soul vibration at work.

And instead of eating and drinking whatever our employer provides, it might be more beneficial to get a selection of teas and nuts and dried fruits and other nourishing treats to enjoy in quiet moments or when we are feeling tired or hungry. We might even consider a little aromatherapy. A collection of favourite oils and a burner can do wonders for the energies around us on the days that don't seem to flow. Alternatively we might feel it is time to get a plant or to reconfigure our office furniture. Why not use the change of season to inspire new touches? Doing these things adds a freshness and a genuine sense of celebration to those spaces where we spend so much of our time.

Making the effort to inject nourishment and inspiration into our days helps lighten our mood and take the edge off our stress. We then find we are more able to take charge of our lives. And when we create a space that is genuinely loving and warm and safe, not only do we benefit – those around us will be drawn to this space and be inspired by it also.

Making the world more beautiful

When we inject more meaning into our lives we also help combat the immense loneliness in the world at large. All too often in this brave new world of ours precious moments slip by unhonoured and unsung. Our towns and cities are full of people battling with the adventure of life.

Countless young couples struggle through the early years of parenthood in isolation, while the elderly feel shut off from the world around them. We cannot make everything right for everyone, but we can at least ease the isolation we encounter by moments of kindness and interest. What we are talking about here is a gentler life filled with far more depth and meaning for our selves and for others.

Rituals to support the various stages of life

In traditional societies each new chapter of life was experienced by the whole community, so everyone was able to benefit from these extraordinary moments. Major life transitions were also dealt with more completely, enabling everyone to learn and to grow by these interactions. Sacred rituals were in place to mark the passage from one stage of life to the next, and to teach those concerned the essence of what it meant to become an adult, to be married, to be pregnant. As a result the transition from one stage of life to the next was not only supported, but better understood. How lacking are our lives by comparison?

I cannot help but feel the reason we have so many difficulties with teenagers today is because they have no rites of passage, no formal help to enable them to make the transition from childhood to being a young adult. Instead they are forced to live in limbo for a number of years. They are constantly told that they are no longer a child but they are not a grown-up either. A definitive answer to this problem is not easy to arrive at, but there have to be certain markers we can put in place to ease their journey and to help them celebrate their growing maturity in more positive ways than are currently available to them and their parents.

Time for men and women to be alone with their kind

More traditional societies encourage men and women to celebrate their differences. Again this is a whole aspect of our lives that has been lost to us. Rarely do we appreciate, let alone embrace, the unique life experience of being a man or a woman. No longer do most of us have access to a sacred sisterhood or brotherhood, yet how much might we gain from new ways of expressing the essentials of who we are and of sharing our accumulated wisdom with each other and with our young? Again we can help by celebrating who we are more fully and by making it safe for others to do likewise. We don't need to form a group, but we can get together now and again with those who feed our souls to celebrate our life's journey.

Honouring our bodies

Often the hectic pace of life allows us little time to be, let alone to be in our bodies, and so we fail to read the signals that former societies understood well. Today many of those who menstruate know well the deep longing for retreat that often arises during this time, yet rarely do we set aside more leisure time than we already have to nurture and support our selves. Once we become conscious of what our body is telling us, we can inject a few simple rituals into our lives to better nurture our selves. Once certain rituals are established, it is a whole lot easier to make the time we need to relax – to take a bath, to be alone, to get to bed early. And we can then support and encourage others to take especial care of themselves at important times in their life cycle also. This is not self-indulgence so much as respecting our own needs.

Honouring our elders

Those who live in more traditional societies value the accumulated wisdom of their elders. Old age is regarded as a culmination, not a diminution, of who one is. In the West, however, the elderly are largely forgotten members of society. Again we must retrace the best of what has been and learn to honour and to nurture those who are our elders.

I am blessed to have a group of older women in my life who lighten my days with their wit and wisdom. We don't all live in the same city or the same country even, but whenever we get together our meetings are joyous and full of laughter, and as we each share our stories we are all enriched. Then when we are done we are able to gather up all magic of these precious moments and bless our lives and the lives of those around us.

Where might your wise old friends be? Perhaps they are in your life already. If so, always be sure that you honour and celebrate them, because they carry with them a great store of wisdom and love and joy.

Rituals for those things that are past

Rituals are as much about death as they are about living. Suggestions as to how we might best deal with death are included in the following chapter. It is worth remembering, however, that we face many deaths in our lives, including the death of relationships. I was heartened to learn of a couple who on separating called family and friends together. When everyone had gathered they publicly acknowledged all that their partner had brought to their lives and honoured them for this. They then blessed each other on the separate journeys that lay ahead, promising to continue to help and care for each other in any way possible. How profound was this ritual, because not only were both individuals able to put the past behind them, they also freed family and friends to have positive relationships with them both.

Similarly when we leave behind a workplace or a home it is always good to give oneself time to be completely alone in this space, so that we can honour all that this place has afforded us and retrieve all the parts of our selves we might have scattered there. And as we feel these parts of our selves returning, we can welcome them back. Then, having bathed our selves and this space in Light, we can complete this little ritual by blessing the space for all who come after us, praying that their experience of this place will be expansive in every sense of the word. When we can do this we bless our lives and the lives of those to come after us by not leaving any psychic garbage behind.

Whatever rituals we dream up, may we do so lightly and joyously, and in celebration of who we are and of this incredible journey we are on. May all that we do be with sacred intent, reflecting the greater truths that underpin all our lives. And in amongst all our commitments, let us not forget that even the most simple moments can be transcendent experiences. They too can touch our hearts and warm our souls.

Contemplations on the opportunities to enrich the moment

Find a place that you love where you can be quiet. Then, as you bring your attention back into your body, take a moment to give thanks for all the blessings you have received in your life – for all the people and places and experiences that have inspired and sustained you. Then, as you feel yourself settle, why not meditate on one or two of the following questions:

- Where is there more joy to be had in my life right now?
- Who are those who make my soul sing, and how best might I celebrate all that they mean to me?
- What forgotten rituals are there within my family or community that might well enrich my days?
- How can this season further enhance my experience and understanding of all that this moment brings to me?
- How can I best complete those chapters of my life that are now past?

Living in the Magic of the Moment

With beauty may I walk.
With beauty before me may I walk.
With beauty behind me may I walk.
With beauty above me may I walk.
With beauty all around me may I walk.
Prayer: 'Night Way'

Always life's beauty waits for us

Opening our selves up to the immeasurable beauty that is already around and inside of us is essential if we are to experience all the deep magic that life has to offer. Yet so distracted are we often that our experience of beauty is a distant one.

Life's exquisite moments are all around us – in nature, in others, in works of art, in the birth of new ideas, in kindness, in selflessness, in joy, in moments of sorrow even. Genuine beauty is like no other – it is yet another face of the Divine. It is there to uplift and sustain us, and to enable us to experience our selves as the expansive beings we are.

Life's beauty waits for that time when we are ready to invite it into our lives. A few years ago I went to see an exhibition on Pompeii, and as I wandered around I was struck by the beauty that was apparent in everything I saw, from the ancient Romans' works of art to their everyday pots and pans. All were decorated with representations of their deities and with fantastic figures of the imagination that delighted the eye and fed the soul. What a contrast this was to the spare nature of our lives, where beauty is a commodity used to sell everything from swimwear to shampoo.

The sacred face of beauty

How little we understand of the intrinsic value of beauty – of its ability to heal and inspire. And what we don't understand, we don't value.

In times past beautiful things were created as an act of devotion to the Sacred. This was the impetus behind countless works of art, behind many of the world's great cathedrals and temples. How much more meaningful our lives and works of creation if instead of seeking to elevate our selves we created something of beauty to honour all that is greater, wiser, and more substantial than we are.

Learning to recognise beauty wherever it might be

If we hope to have an authentic relationship with beauty, we need to learn how to recognise and appreciate it wherever we find it. It is easy to touch life's beauty when we are in a place or with people that uplift us, but if we wish to embrace all the beauty that life offers, we must look beyond the obvious.

Then we discover that even amongst the noise and pollution of our cities, in good times and bad, there beauty resides also. We see it all around us – from the plant that struggles up between the cracks in the pavement, to the faint breeze that takes the heat off a stifling summer's day. When we can recognise these many delicious nuances in everyday life and give thanks for them, we are able to enjoy a more intimate relationship with life's sacred beauty no matter where we are.

The Transformative Power of Beauty

Beauty has the capacity not only to uplift and inspire us, but also to teach us a great deal. It takes the mundane and transforms it, so that we too can begin to see the extraordinary contained in those things that at a first glance seem ordinary. Then, as we look even more deeply, we discover that everything is not so much ordinary or extraordinary as complete in its own way.

When we allow beauty to inspire and teach us, to help make us complete, we learn to live lightly, to be awake to all that each moment holds. And once beauty becomes an integral part of who we are and everything we do, our life experience deepens. We start to live each and every moment of our lives. We start to discern life's beauty in times of joy and of suffering – in those profound moments when we are with a loved one whose life is slipping away, or when someone feels safe enough to be vulnerable with us. When we are able to appreciate the beauty that resides in the midst of pain and sorrow even, we discover life at its most meaningful.

These extraordinarily beautiful moments are sent to heal those parts of us that are broken and to enrich who we are in essence. They can and do strengthen our sense of purpose and our vision. They inspire us to live more creatively – to open our selves up to all the possibilities that are available to us.

In times long gone the stranger at the gate was honoured, because it was believed the gods walked amongst us. This is a profound understanding, because every time we reach out to those who come into our lives unannounced, there the Divine is also. When we can embrace this expansive way of living, how exquisite are the many possibilities for our lives.

When we allow our selves to be sustained by the sacred beauty of life, we no longer experience a terrible emptiness inside. No longer do we postpone opportunities for happiness until we have our first home or first child, our new partner or new drapes. Still we strive to achieve, but we also recognise that good, bad or indifferent, each moment has something to offer and to teach us about our selves and the world around us, and it is through these in-sights we become wise.

Creating beauty in and around us

As we start to make life's magic our own, we realise our life's quest is not only to discover and appreciate all the beauty we can find, but to look for opportunities to *create* these qualities in our lives. This means inviting beauty and goodness into spaces where none seems to exist. This might well take courage, but when we do seize the moment and invite beauty in, not only do we create a better space for our selves and others, we discover the many talents we carry within as well.

Some years ago our office space was reorganised and I ended up in the most depressing part of the building with old furniture and little natural light. This wasn't what I had hoped for, yet I quickly realised that if I wanted something done about it, it was up to me. I cleaned every surface, then smudged my workspace, asking that it bless all who entered. I then bought some plants and uplifting prints and within days the energy in my office was transformed. Even though nothing had been done about the lighting or the furniture, everything was noticeably brighter. Frequently people would comment on what a great spot I had to work in, and they were right, because it was a space devoted to Love and Light.

So when we find things not to our liking, instead of giving up or waiting to be rescued, we need to recognise that this might well be the perfect opportunity for us to take charge of our lives and to put into practice those things we hold dear. When we do this we take back our power by inviting those things that are beautiful and sacred to be with us in all that we do, and then not only do we nurture every level of our being, we become wiser also.

When we free our selves from the limitations of living solely in our heads, we rediscover whole aspects of our selves we had forgotten about. We begin to experience what it means to be truly alive in mind, body and spirit. With this heightened sense of aliveness comes the deep joy of knowing that we can embrace life's beauty and mystery wherever we are.

Honouring our creativity

These days many of us are uncomfortable with things of the heart. The more technologically orientated our world becomes, the more removed we are from many of the things that allow us to express who we really are. When we abandon these fundamental aspects of our selves, we end up living with ideas and values that are not our own, and then we wonder why our world seems so alien so much of the time.

Today there is little room left for personal expression. Rarely do we have the opportunity to paint or weave, to make paper or pottery, or to turn wood. We are all very busy, but the reason for our loss of creativity isn't just a question of time. So self-conscious have we become that we are afraid to be our selves, and so we end up living someone else's vision.

When we do have the courage to embrace the magic of who we are, we liberate our selves from all those things that limit us. When we are at home with who we are and what we do, we are then able to celebrate our uniqueness body and soul, and to allow others to do likewise.

A return to intimacy and nurture

In the fast pace of contemporary life, much that feeds us has been sacrificed for efficiency, when what our world needs is all the inspiration and intimacy we can bring to our lives to make us whole. I still remember the profound joy as a child when my mother made my favourite meal, because it fed every part of me. Whenever my aunts and grandmother knitted for me, this too was a wonderful experience. I can still recall the thrill of being measured, of first seeing the wool that had been chosen, and then watching the patterns take shape. When finally the garments were finished I went about my childhood days cocooned in their love. These are intimate acts, which not only warm but transform our lives.

Sadly these opportunities for creativity and deep soulfulness are in danger of slipping away from us. Let us hope this does not happen. Whenever my sister and I get together at her home, what I love most are the moments we share over a meal she has made. These loving gestures are vital forms of self-expression that bind us to each other, that add colour and depth to our days. When we lose our chance to add our unique touch to life, we lose the chance to give our lives shape and form, and above all meaning.

Nurturing self-expression in our little ones

Our children come into this world bursting with creativity. They put their hearts and souls into all that they do, giving those around them an immense amount of pleasure. Then as they start to take on different values this capacity fades. They become self-conscious, aware that while they might be good at drawing or writing, they might never get their work shown in a gallery, or they might not be published. Knowing the store that adults set by such things they feel diminished, and so they stop creating the very things they love, and as they do so something vital inside them dies.

This story is familiar to us all, because at some level this is our story. Yet it is not too late to rediscover all that we are capable of. We can still come home from work and fling paint on a canvas. We can still take up woodwork or needlework or photography or whatever our passion might be. When we do these things joyously and unselfconsciously, we can fully express all those things inside us that have been left unsaid. And as we give our selves permission to be who we are, to experience the magic that is ours, then we are more able to give others the inspiration and the support to do likewise.

Embracing the beauty of the moment

One of the greatest threats to embracing the beauty of our self-expression and the wider beauty around us is our frenetic lifestyles. So busy have we become that often we end up living somewhere outside of our selves. If we are not careful these manic habits spill over into our leisure time, allowing us little space to reflect or to be. When we are on holiday or in places that are special, we are so busy writing our journal or taking photos that we can't absorb the moment. And then, sadly, all the spellbinding layers of a particular location are lost to us.

Of course we can take photos or write postcards, but what we need most is to gather up all the magic these moments offer and bury them deep in our hearts, so that we can carry them with us wherever we go. When we can absorb all the beauty and truth we are able, our lives are transformed, because we *become* that beauty, that truth.

One afternoon I was having a sandwich in a nearby park when in an instant the grass became greener than anything I had ever experienced. So green was the grass that it was like experiencing a whole new colour. This astonishing moment expanded and I then experienced the life force in each and every one of these hundreds upon hundreds of individual blades of grass. So active were they that they were literally shimmering with life. I was transfixed as their aliveness coursed through me. This was an experience of the one-ness of all living things that was far beyond anything I had previously encountered. I will never forget the transcendent beauty of being able to experience the life force in this way.

I cannot explain why this experience was mine, or why it happened when it did, other than it deepened my appreciation of the miracle of life immeasurably. Over the years I have come to realise that part of the deep joy of the human quest is the capacity to savour such moments, to yield to their fullness, and to simply allow their mystery to unfold.

And so as we strive to gather up all of life's magic and beauty, may we each begin to seek those things in our lives that align us with the Sacred. May we begin to challenge our selves with new ideas and with new ways of doing things, in the knowledge that everything we undertake has the capacity to reflect and enhance the Divine in life. May we also realise that as we embrace all that is beautiful and sacred, we are embracing the source of our strength and wisdom as well.

A prayer for beauty

'O, Great Spirit, help me to reach out and touch the beauty that is within and around me. Help me to see the beauty in those things that are obvious and in those things that are not. Give me the courage to invite beauty into those places where none seems to exist, so that always I might honour the Sacred Presence and Beauty in all things.'

About Death

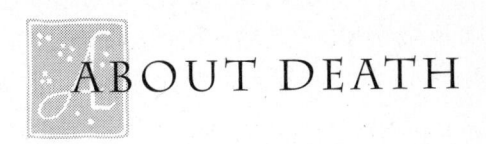

DEATH IS NOT A ONE-OFF EXPERIENCE
These days we not only avoid death, we tend to live our lives as if death doesn't exist. Yet while who we are in essence never dies, we will all leave our bodies and this plane of existence behind, so we need to be prepared for this eventuality. For many death is a fearful notion, but if we are to truly appreciate earthly life in its fullness and beauty, we need to understand all that death can bring to our lives.

One of the reasons we are unable to handle the whole prospect of death is that we have let go of the many rituals that enabled us to say goodbye, that helped us adjust to life without the deceased, and we are the poorer for this. The best kind of rituals reach the hearts of all concerned, bringing peace and calm, and enabling us to understand more about death.

The very mention of death evokes all sorts of emotions, yet already we have died a thousand deaths. Each day of our lives old cells perish and new cells are born, and like the snake we too shed many skins on our journey through life. We do this as we grow and mature, as our passions and our priorities alter, when our life circumstances change.

In looking at all the people and friendships, all the jobs and places we have experienced, we begin to realise that our lives are in a constant state of evolution. We are not the person we were five years ago. Often we are not even the person we were a year or six months ago. When we look back over our life, sometimes it is as if we are looking at the lives of half a dozen completely different people. Some of the transitions we made from being one kind of person to the next were smooth, while some were less so. Even now there are aspects of our lives that will wither and die, but along with this are a whole new set of possibilities yet to be born.

Death is merely the shedding of yet another skin

Once we realise death is merely a particular point in the vastness of time and space, we can start to look at it differently. This doesn't mean death is unimportant – it is a vitally important part of our soul journey. It is, however, nothing to be frightened of. The more we embrace the Sacred, the more we realise that even though we will experience death and loss, nothing is ever taken from us that will not ultimately enhance our lives. Again we can only come to a deep understanding of this universal law when we make the time to explore the texture and nuances of this understanding, and to embrace its practical wisdom as well.

Knowing when something is over

One of the great instincts we learn as we embrace the Sacred is to recognise when something is at an end, and to face this moment without any judgement. This might be the end of a friendship or a job or a life. Even though we might feel sad at these endings, as we progress we learn to have enough faith in the universe to know that the more we are able to let go of those things that are past, the more we are able to move towards the many people and experiences that still await us. We learn to trust the process, knowing that whatever direction we are being guided in is for our highest good.

When we can recognise this and respond accordingly, letting go becomes a way of life that brings an even greater lightness of being. So every time we are able to let go of those things that are fading from our lives, the greater our sense of meaning will be, and the greater our capacity to learn and to grow.

Uncertainty around death only arises when our view of our selves is incomplete – when we see our selves purely in terms of flesh and blood. When our lives are preoccupied with the material realm, we cling to what we can touch and count and label. Then, when we are faced with death we are devastated. Yet in spite of all we might fear, our sacred essence is with us throughout our earthly lives and beyond it. Just as it is appropriate to leave certain things behind when we make a transition from one part of our lives to next, so too the soul sheds its body at the conclusion of our time on Earth, so that it can continue its ongoing adventure through time and space.

When we fear death, we fear life

The journey through life and beyond it was never meant to be a fearful experience, but for many it seems terrifying, and because they can't control it, they avoid it altogether. Dying has become so removed from our lives as to be almost invisible, and what we don't understand we fear.

This view has contributed to the breakdown of our relationship with the elderly. In our great desire to avoid the inevitability of death, we ignore those who are approaching the end of their lives. So instead of being honoured for their wealth of experience, the elderly are forgotten, and their wisdom and in-sight are lost to future generations.

How often within our own families do we mourn the loss of an elderly relative, wishing that we had had more contact, wishing that we had taken greater interest in them and their stories? The secret is to cherish those in our lives right now, be they young or old, because when we do so we are able to live fully and without regret.

Being with those who are dying

Often when we are faced with the prospect of being with someone who is dying it can be frightening, because this is an unfamiliar situation. We worry about our reactions and our ability to cope, not realising we are being given the opportunity to enter an extraordinary space. This space might well demand a great deal of us, but it is also a profoundly sacred space that will bring us immense blessings. If instead of getting lost in our fears we simply hold in our hearts the Light of all the good and beautiful things that this person means to us, we will be far better equipped to journey into the unfamiliar territory between this life and the next.

Understanding the sacred gifts that dying moments bring

I can still remember the first time I was faced with being there for a friend who was dying. I desperately wanted to make sure that my friend, Nick, got all the love and support he deserved, especially as he was dying of AIDS and there was so much fear about this illness at the time.

Being with Nick didn't bother me, because I had no fear of death, yet when the time came to see him I was terrified, because

I was worried about how I would cope. What if I cried? What if he could see my shock? And what if everything I said sounded empty or, even worse, like false optimism? I wanted to give Nick all the support I was capable of, but I was desperately concerned that I didn't have what he needed to help him through this time.

I can still recall how hard my heart was beating as I made my way down the hospital corridor. Everything inside me wanted to turn tail and run, but the moment I saw Nick my fears evaporated. My heart opened to see a person who had been so full of life scarcely able to lift his hand. Yet even in his weakened state, all the things I loved about Nick remained. As I sat with him over his remaining weeks, I loved our times together. I came to realise that I was merely a conduit for a quality of Love and Light that was far beyond anything I could give. I yielded to the process, and these moments proved to be some of the most beautiful moments of my entire life.

Over the days and weeks that followed I was privileged to enter the deeply sacred space that lies in and around death. As I ventured into this awesome space I realised that I had reached a place like no other. There were moments when I felt the presence of the Great Spirit so tangibly I felt It occupying every part of me.

As Nick grew closer to death, so much of what had been part of his life and personality dropped away, and little by little I was able to see the divine essence of the one I knew as Nick. I was able to observe and to honour the sacred spark around which his personality and his idiosyncrasies had grown.

Still there were times when Nick was in terrible pain, when I longed to relieve him of his agony. In these moments all I could do was be strong for him by adjusting his pillows and giving him a drink, by holding his hand and telling him how much I loved him.

We simply stayed with each other in the moment, yielding to the now and to all that it gave us.

Each day I left the hospital a different person. So much of what had seemed important was suddenly of no importance at all, and those things that had seemed peripheral came into sharp focus. I felt more alive, more clear about life than I had done in a long time. In amongst all the pain were many humorous moments as well – sent no doubt to help us through.

Beyond our fears lies a profoundly sacred space

As we each face the prospect of being with someone who is dying, it is important we know that in amongst dealing with the welter of emotions, we have the opportunity to enter one of the most profound experiences that life can offer us. By tending our loved one, we are enabling every aspect of ourselves to be stretched beyond what we thought we were capable of, and beyond what we thought life and death were about.

When we allow our selves to step beyond our fears and preconceptions of how things should or should not be, and simply open our selves up to the situation, we will begin to understand the impact of what we are able to do for another when we remain in the present moment. We will discover that, instead of trying to control the process, when we yield our selves to each moment and simply be there for another and hold a good space for them, our contribution to their soul's transition can be a profound one. As we do so we too will learn more about life and about the mystery of death than we could ever have imagined.

We are never alone

As we deal with the inevitable hurt of losing someone we love, of seeing them in pain and of watching them slip slowly away, we are reminded that we do not take this journey alone. Always we are in the presence of the Great Spirit, who will continue to surround us with Light and Love, as long as we remember to ask for it. Many other beings of Light also surround us at this time, guiding us and supporting us to help our loved one onto the next stage of their journey.

As much as part of us might wish for our loved one to remain, always we must be mindful of their higher good. We must allow them to move on when they are ready, because their life is in the hands of the Great Spirit, not ours. Often we assume that if we had prayed long and hard enough, or if we had done things differently, we could have helped snatch those we love from the jaws of death. We only feel this way because of our sense of helplessness, and because we do not understand the wider picture.

The journey our loved one is on is a journey through lifetimes, each of which has its own set of adventures – its joys and disappointments and lessons. Just because their time on Earth has drawn to a close, it is no cause for us to feel desperate. We help those who are dying best by honouring and supporting them as they get ready to take on life's next adventure.

Ensuring our loved ones die in peace

The quieter and more peaceful the environment around the person who is passing the better, because they need all the physical, mental and spiritual space they can get in preparation for the journey ahead. Sometimes it might be appropriate to talk to them. Whether or not they are conscious doesn't matter, because still they are able to take in what we are saying. When we do talk always we must do so positively and peacefully, and in a way that reflects back to them their divine magnificence and all the many wonderful things they have done with their lives. Whatever we say must be done to calm and comfort them, and to allow them to move on.

Often it might seem appropriate to talk, but equally there are times when there is no room for words. No matter what state they are in, our loved ones can still benefit from the loving energy we send them. It will comfort their souls and light their way. We can do this by simply holding a space of Light for them as we give them our love. Again we do so without trying to hold on to them in any way. If our loved one is afraid to let go, we can call upon the Great Spirit's help to smooth their passage and fill their journey with Love and Light. Then, as we seek to reassure them, we can also give them permission to let go.

Saying goodbye

Sometimes we are able to be with the one we love until they pass over, and sometimes they slip away from us without warning. We must never be disappointed if we haven't had the chance to say goodbye, because our ability to communicate with those who have passed over remains. All we need do is reach out to them by conversing with them or by saying a prayer on their behalf. Either way we can tell them all that is in our hearts and bless them on their journey. And in so doing we relieve our selves of emotions that are not helpful to us, and release our loved one to their highest good.

If we can't be with our loved one physically on their departure, we can still light a candle and pray for them, knowing that whatever Love and Light we send forth will flow through the cosmos, warming and encouraging our loved one and lighting their way. Even kind and supportive thoughts can have a profound effect on the passage of that soul.

When the person who has passed away is a close family

member or a dear friend, it can be immensely healing to visit them prior to the funeral. This might at first seem a daunting prospect, but when we can do this, we are more capable of completing this stage of our relationship with them. We are also better able to understand the difference between body and spirit, because we will see clearly that all that lies before us is the empty shell, and that the person we love has well and truly departed.

As our loved ones step beyond this life, they embrace new dimensions of being. If we really want to help them, we must always pray for the advancement of their soul, asking that they will continue to journey on to an outcome that will be for their highest good. We must also remember that they cannot only see us, they can also feel what we feel. Knowing this we can take comfort from the fact that even when our loved ones have passed over, they are not lost to us.

With this knowledge comes responsibility. If we allow our selves to drown in sorrow, our grief will touch them – they will experience our hurt. Similarly when our lives are joyous, we are able to bring them our joy. So if we truly love those we have lost, we have to release them from the grip of our emotions, so that always we can bless them with our joy and gratitude.

One of the hardest aspects of losing someone we love is that all we have to attend to doesn't stop when the person has died. Living in a death-denying society doesn't help us cope with the possibility of death, let alone with the practicalities of funerals and so on. How do we find the words to articulate all a person has meant to us? How do we acknowledge their passing appropriately? Again our inner guidance will serve us well, particularly when we remember that as painful as these times are, this is only a temporary farewell, not a final parting. At the end of this chapter is a eulogy that might help shape your words for such an occasion.

Expressing our condolences

Often when someone passes away we want to try to soften the blow, but we feel unable to find the right expression for our condolences, and so we end up sending flowers and a card. We turn up to the funeral, if we are able, and then we concentrate on trying to help the bereaved person get their life back to normal.

If instead of simply signing a bereavement card, we take a few moments to add our own heartfelt message, it will mean a great deal. If we are able to write a letter, then better still. More than likely these words will be read over and over in the weeks and months ahead, and will provide ongoing sustenance to the bereaved person. Flowers are lovely, but why not consider buying the bereaved person a photo frame, so that they can have a favourite photo of their loved one to hand? The gift of a commemorative plant or tree is also a beautiful touch. Making a meal or offering to organise groceries can often be of most value, because still the daily aspects of life need attending to and can prove burdensome to those who are dealing with their loss.

Allowing grief to run its course

As time passes it is right and good that we encourage the bereaved person to begin to pick up the pieces, but we cannot force the process. Before they can move on they have to be able to grieve and to find their own way to come to terms with their loss. For some this might be a relatively short period, while for others it can take many months or years even. The more we try to nudge the bereaved person on, the more we fail to allow them to be in their own space. When we are impatient to have them move forward, we need to ask our selves whether it is the bereaved person's sorrow or our own discomfort we are most concerned about.

All too often those who have lost someone are devastated by the inability of friends and relatives to deal with their grief. This unwillingness to talk about the deceased condemns the bereaved person to silence, causing them to feel even more isolated and lost. So while the very mention of the person who has passed over might feel awkward and might precipitate tears, when done with love and sensitivity it can do much to aid the healing process for all concerned.

One of the hardest areas to face is the loss of a child. This situation is often so devastating that we cannot take it in. Yet even though we might struggle with what to say, we must allow the parents to talk about their child and to continue to make them part of their lives, so that over time they can move on. When we can step beyond our own discomfort, we are more able to assist others in their bereavement.

Often it isn't the immediate days subsequent to the death and funeral that are the hardest, but those that follow, when support for the bereaved person is slowly withdrawn. And while the bereaved person might seem to be coping, appearances can be deceptive. The quiet times can prove the most agonising for those left behind. One moment all is well, and the next the bereaved person is overwhelmed by a grief that seems to have no end. This is normal. We cannot love someone and allow them to be part of our lives, then simply pretend they never existed.

Kindness heals

When a person is struggling with their grief, often simple acts of kindness can save the day. A dear friend who recently lost her husband is constantly heartened by the kindness of a neighbour who calls to see her every Sunday morning with a freshly baked croissant. This friend doesn't stay long, but it is the fact that he bothers to drop by, to be kind, that matters. We can all think of our own ways to warm the lives of those who grieve, and while we cannot take away their pain, we can ease their moments with loving-kindness.

Over time it is easy to forget about the passing of friends and family altogether. Another friend who lost her husband in tragic circumstances some years ago is touched by the fact that several close friends and colleagues still make the time to contact her on or around the anniversary of her husband's death. When we take time to partake in these simple gestures, we honour the preciousness of all that has been and all that we can still enjoy.

Keeping the memory of loved ones alive

Marking the lives of those who are no longer with us is important for our own sake as well as for those who have passed over. I was greatly blessed as a child to go with my grandmother and great-aunt to the local cemetery to tend the family graves. As we went about our simple tasks they would tell me about the lives of those whose graves we were tending. Even though most family members had died long before I was born, it gave me a strong sense of context, and to this very day I love to walk through old graveyards and to linger over the headstones.

The more we can embrace the reality of death and celebrate it as the next great adventure, the richer and more meaningful all our lives will be. This is something that we can do not only for ourselves, but for our children also. Even if there are no family graves nearby, we can still have photos of our loved ones and make those who have departed part of our everyday lives.

Too often those who have passed over disappear from sight. My uncle has a wonderful framed collage of family photos that spans decades, and whenever we visit we spend time looking at the photos, savouring the happy moments we have shared with those who are still with us and with those who have passed over. By becoming more familiar with those who died before we were born, we are more able to make them part of our lives. As we observe this collection of individuals and all that they did or did not do with their lives, they have much to teach us as well. They give us a greater sense of belonging, enriching who we are and what we are part of. And we in turn can bless them with our loving thoughts and light their way with an occasional prayer.

A friend who spent Christmas in Finland some years back was thrilled by their Christmas Eve custom of honouring their dead. Friends and family place poinsettias and candles on the graves of those they have lost. Imagine the sight of a snow-covered cemetery brought to life by the blazing red of the poinsettias and the flicker of hundreds of candles. What a beautiful way to begin Christmas by remembering those we love.

There is nothing to fear in death

It is curious that we spend so much of our time agonising over the end of our earthly life, yet give little or no thought to what happened before we came here. To say death is a doorway might sound trite, but this is the case. Death is our great release, our opportunity to go home.

As we contemplate our life's journey, it is worth remembering that even when we have forgotten about our sacred selves, it doesn't mean they cease to exist. Our divine essence is indestructible. It is the spark that fires the life within us, that knows no end. And even though we might not fully understand the completion of our life's quest, we can rest assured there is no need for us to be fearful.

When we take time to be still we are able to see who we are beyond our physical bodies. We are given the opportunity to get to know our selves in the entirety of our mind, body and spirit, and to discover how awesome we are as beings. We see who we are in essence, then we come to realise that this part of us is not only real and living, but that it will never die.

A eulogy

Frequently we feel lost when asked to deliver a eulogy. This might help you find the words you need to express your own thoughts and feelings:

'Our dear, beloved Jonathan, you have been and will always remain a part of our lives.

'You have lived a life that was good and full. You have lived with passion and compassion. Treasured husband to Tara, treasured uncle to Jim and Anna, and treasured by all of us, your extended family, we honour you.

'Yours has been an extraordinary life. You came to us in the guise of someone quite ordinary, concealing your exceptional talents in everyday acts of kindness. Yet like all those who hold the deep magic of life, you transformed the everyday and made the mundane special for us.

'Jonathan, you will live on larger than life in our hearts and minds, but more than this we know you live on in your own right and that is our great comfort.

'And now, dear friend, as you gently close this chapter and set off for landscapes and dimensions we can only dream about, we send you all our love – love greater than you have ever imagined.

'Travel well, dear friend, and sooner or later we look forward to seeing you again and finding out what you've been up

to, because we know that when it's our turn to journey across the great divide you'll be there to welcome us.

'Now, we are off to further celebrate your life and all that we shared with you. Today, Jonathan, is your day and we love and bless you for it.'

COMING HOME

A blessing for your journey
May the Great Spirit bless you and keep you and all you love as you journey home.

Recommended Further Reading

Bek, Lilla, with Pullar, Philippa, *To the Light*, Mandala Books, Allen & Unwin, 1985

Braden, Gregg, *Walking Between the Worlds: The science of compassion*, Radio Bookstore Press, Washington, 1997

Brunton, Paul, *A Search in Secret India*, Rider, London, 1970

Brunton, Paul, *The Secret Path: A technique of spiritual self-discovery for the modern world*, Rider, London, 1969

Brunton, Paul, *The Wisdom of the Overself*, Rider, London, 1969

Dent, Margaret, *Love Never Dies: Extraordinary accounts of survival beyond death*, Bantam Books, Sydney, 1999

Elias, Jason, and Ketcham, Katherine, *In the House of the Moon: Reclaiming the feminine spirit of healing*, Hodder and Stoughton, Sydney, 1995

Jung, C. J, *Memories, Dreams, Reflections*, Pantheon Books, New York, 1973

Linn, Denise, *Sacred Space: Clearing and enhancing the energy of your home*, Rider, London, 1995

Moody, Raymond, *Life After Life: The investigation of a phenomenon – survival of bodily death*, Rider, London, 2001

Muktananda Paramahansa, Swami, *I Have Become Alive:*

Secrets of the inner journey, Siddha Yoga Foundation, Melbourne, 1985

Muktananda Paramahansa, Swami, *Where Are You Going: A guide to the spiritual journey*, Siddha Yoga Foundation, Melbourne, 1985

O'Donohue, John, *Anam Cara*, Bantam Press, London, 1997

Osborne, Arthur, *Ramana Maharshi and the Path of Self Knowedge*, Rider, London, 1974

Sutherland, Cherie, *Children of the Light*, Bantam Books, Sydney, 1995

Sutherland, Cherie, *Transformed by the Light: Life after near-death experiences*, Bantam Books, Sydney, 1992

Sutherland, Cherie, *Within the Light: Twenty remarkable accounts of near-death experiences and how they changed people's lives*, Bantam Books, Sydney, 1993.

Very, Thomas, with Kelly, John, *The Secret Life of the Unborn Child: A remarkable and controversial look at life before birth*, Sphere, London, 1982

Villoldo, Alberto, *Healer, Shaman, Sage: How to heal yourself and others with the energy medicine of the Americas*, Harmony Books, New York, 2000

Wambach, Helen, *Life Before Life*, Bantam Books, New York, 1979

White Eagle, *The Quiet Mind, Sayings of White Eagle*, White Eagle Publishing Trust, Liss, Hampshire, England, 1972.

White, Ian, *Australian Bush Flower Essences*, Bantam Books, Sydney, 1997

White, Ian, *Australian Bush Flower Healing*, Bantam Books, Sydney, 1999

Worwood, Valerie Ann, *Fragrant Heavens: The spiritual*

Recommended further reading

dimension of fragrance and aromatherapy, Bantam Books, London, 1999

Worwood, Valerie Ann, *Fragrant Mind: Aromatherapy for personality, mind, mood and emotion*, Bantam Books, London, 1997

Worwood, Valerie Ann, *Fragrant Pharmacy: A complete guide to aromatherapy and essential oils*, Bantam Books, London, 1991

Yogananda Paramahansa, *Autobiography of a Yogi*, Self-realization Fellowship, Los Angeles, 1985

Yogananda Paramahansa, *Man's Eternal Quest*, Self-realization Fellowship, Los Angeles, 1982

NOTES FOR YOUR PERSONAL JOURNEY

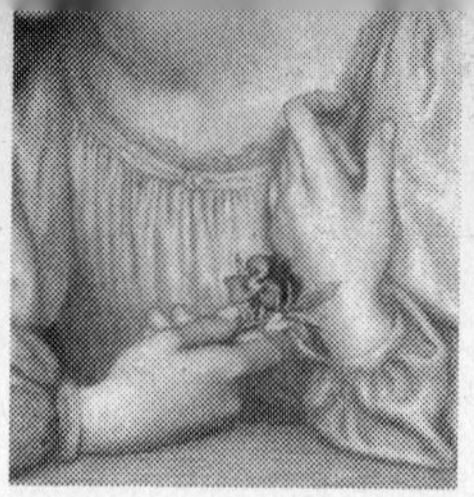

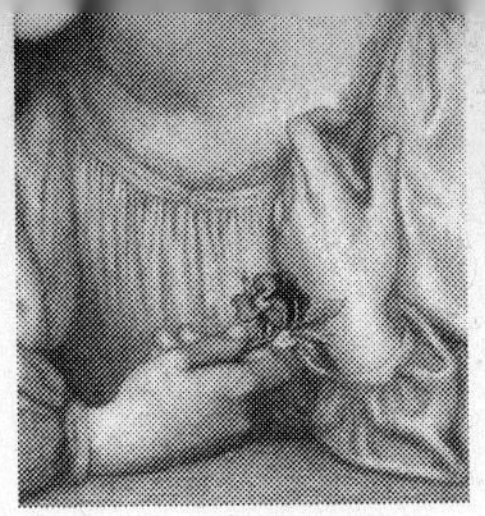

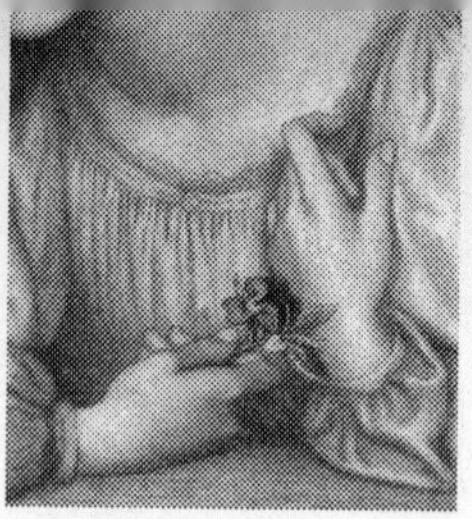

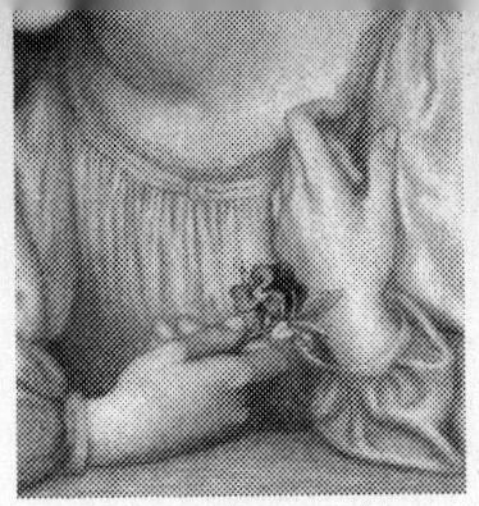

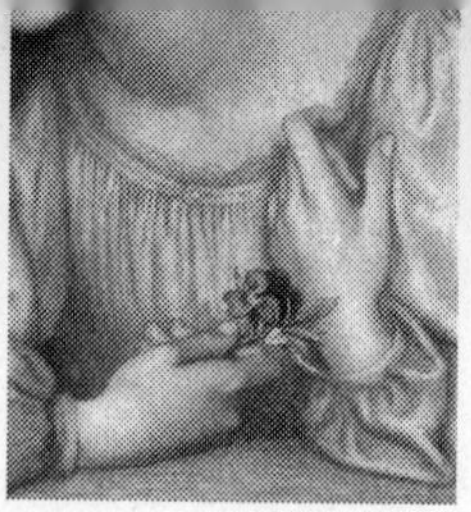

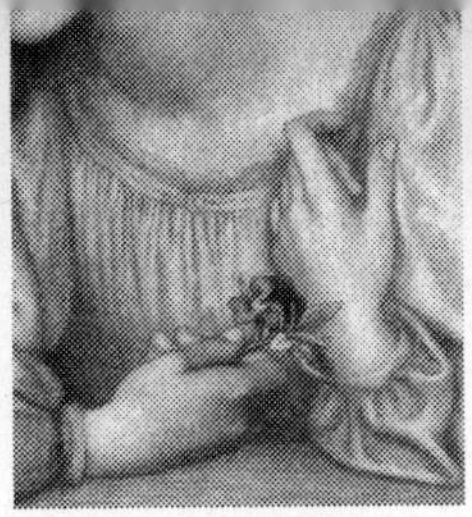

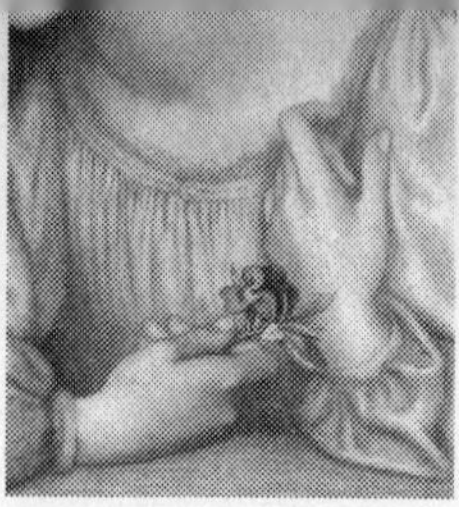